AF333264

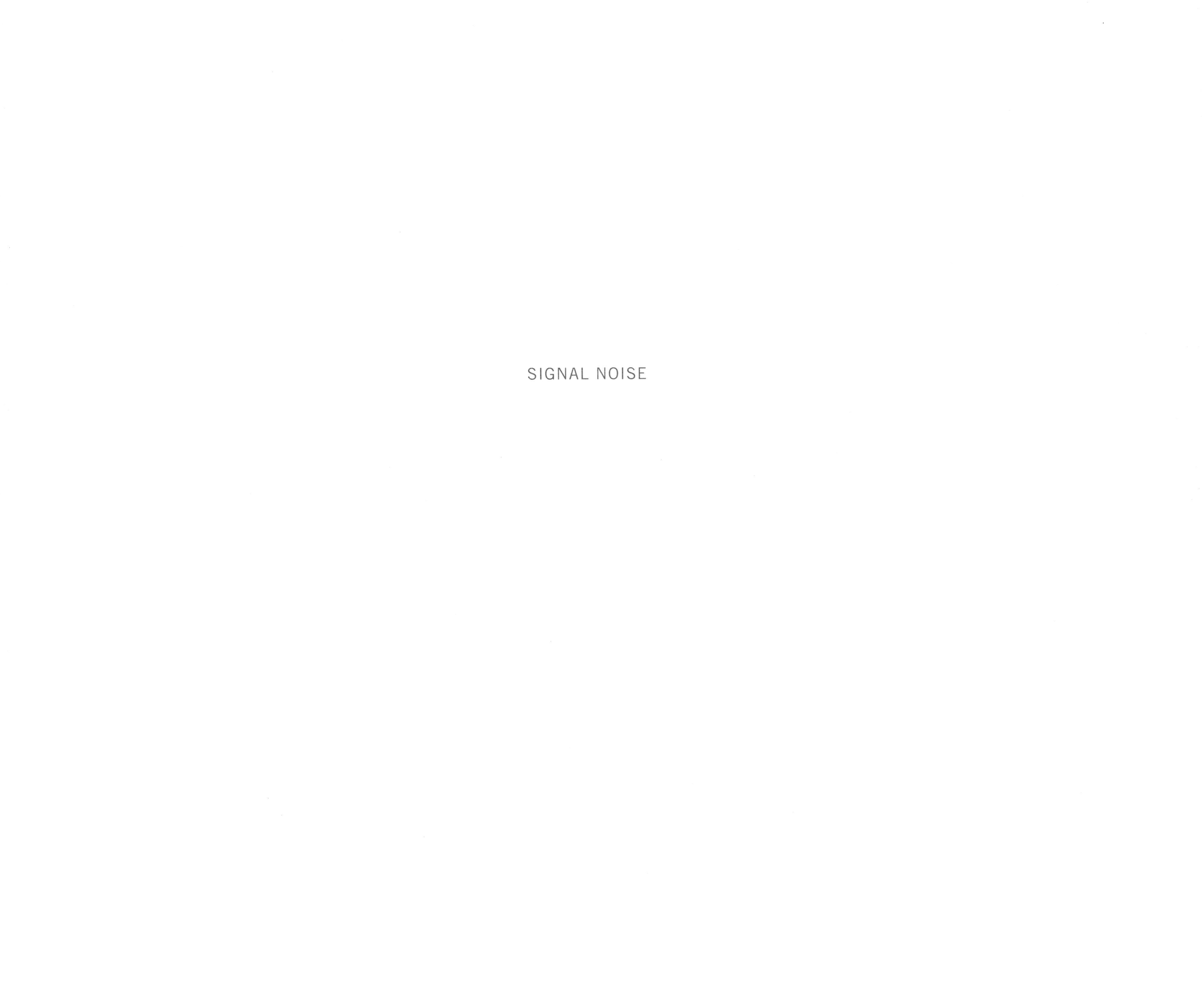

SIGNAL NOISE

SIGNAL NOISE

Aaron Rothman

RADIUS BOOKS

"… Fundamentally it is neither thing seen only
 nor seer only, it is visibility sometimes wandering
 and sometimes reassembled."

— MAURICE MERLEAU-PONTY
The Visible and the Invisible

"There was a shopping mall
 Now it's all covered with flowers
 You've got it, you've got it
 If this is paradise
 I wish I had a lawnmower
 You've got it, we've got it"

— TALKING HEADS
(Nothing But) Flowers

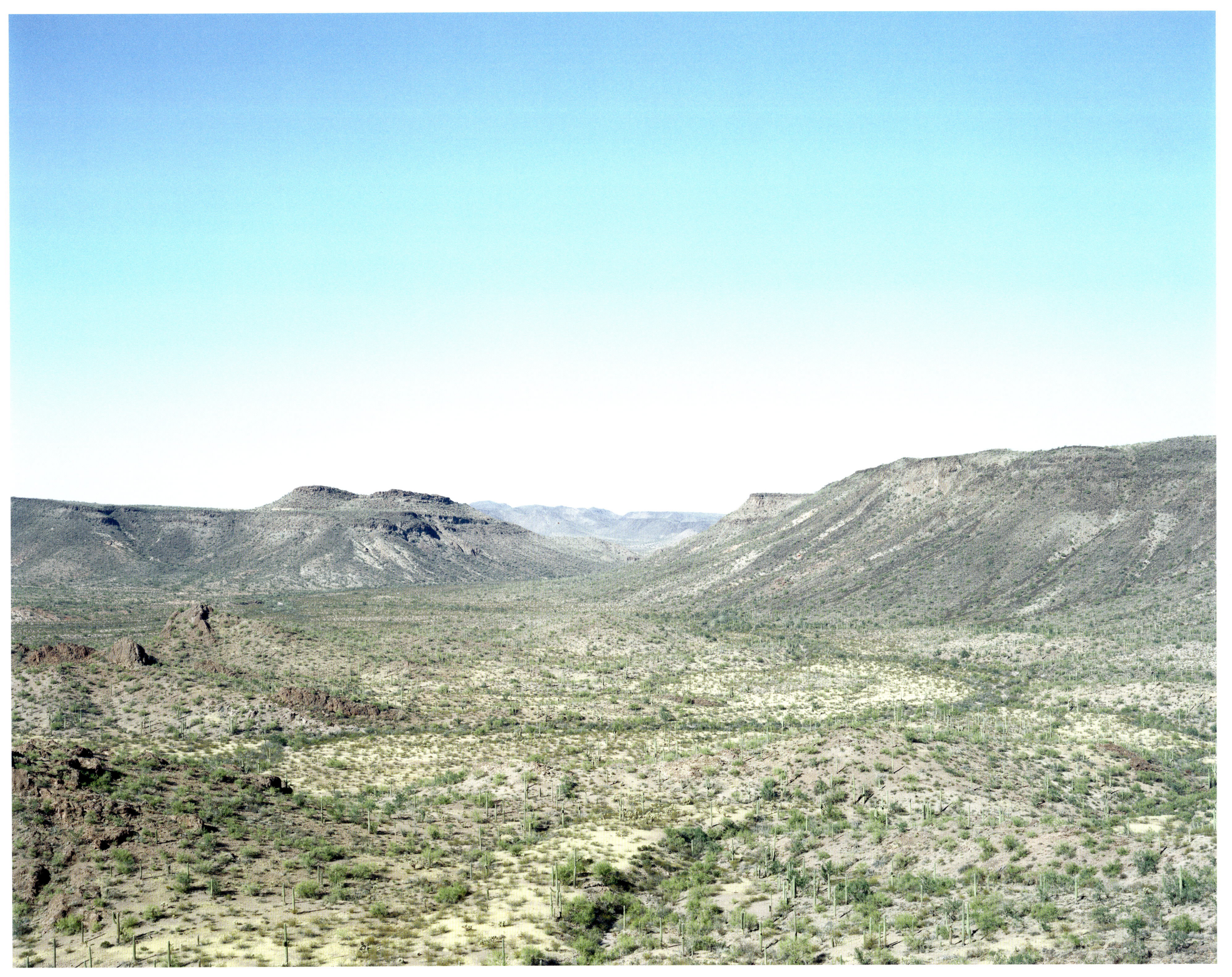

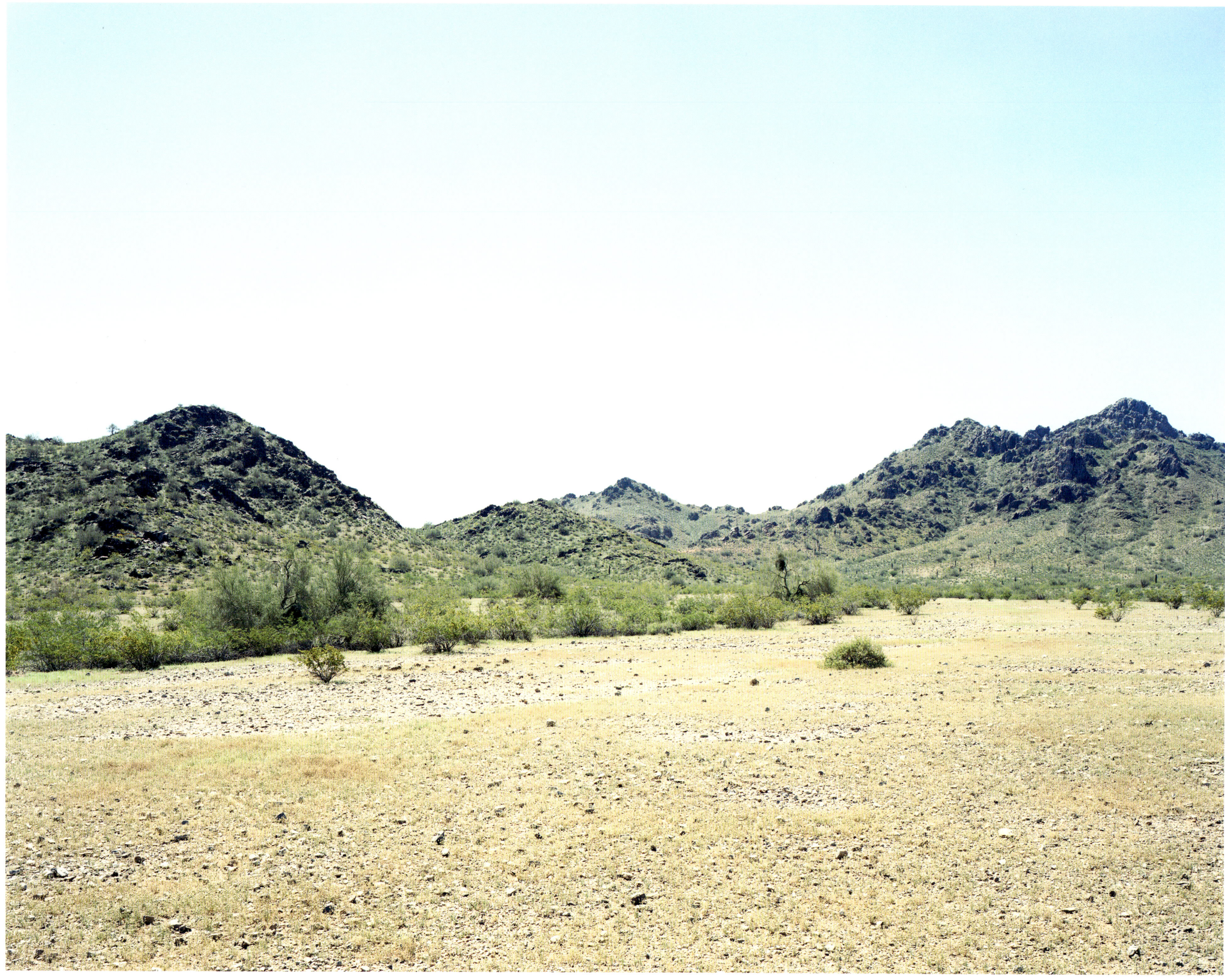

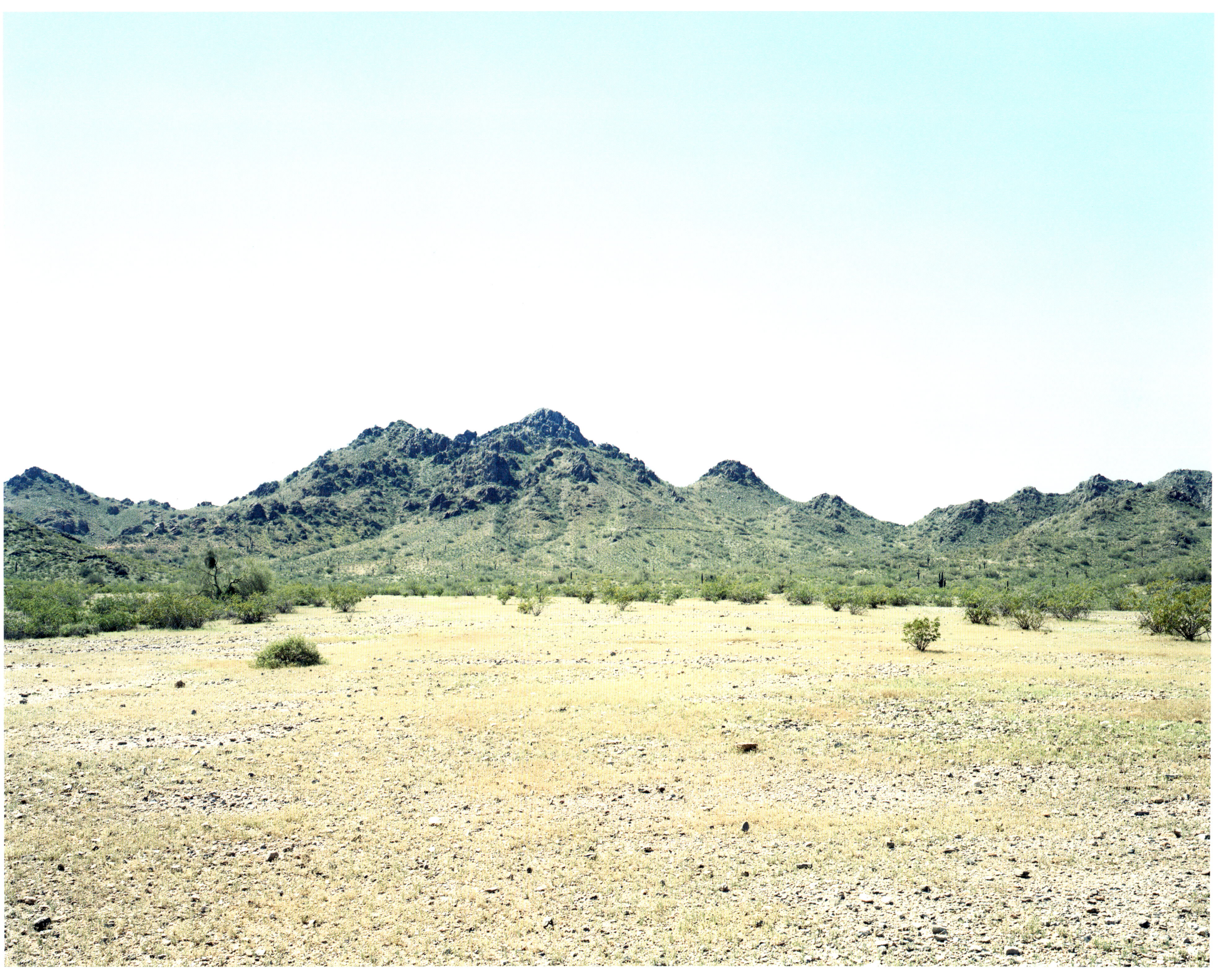

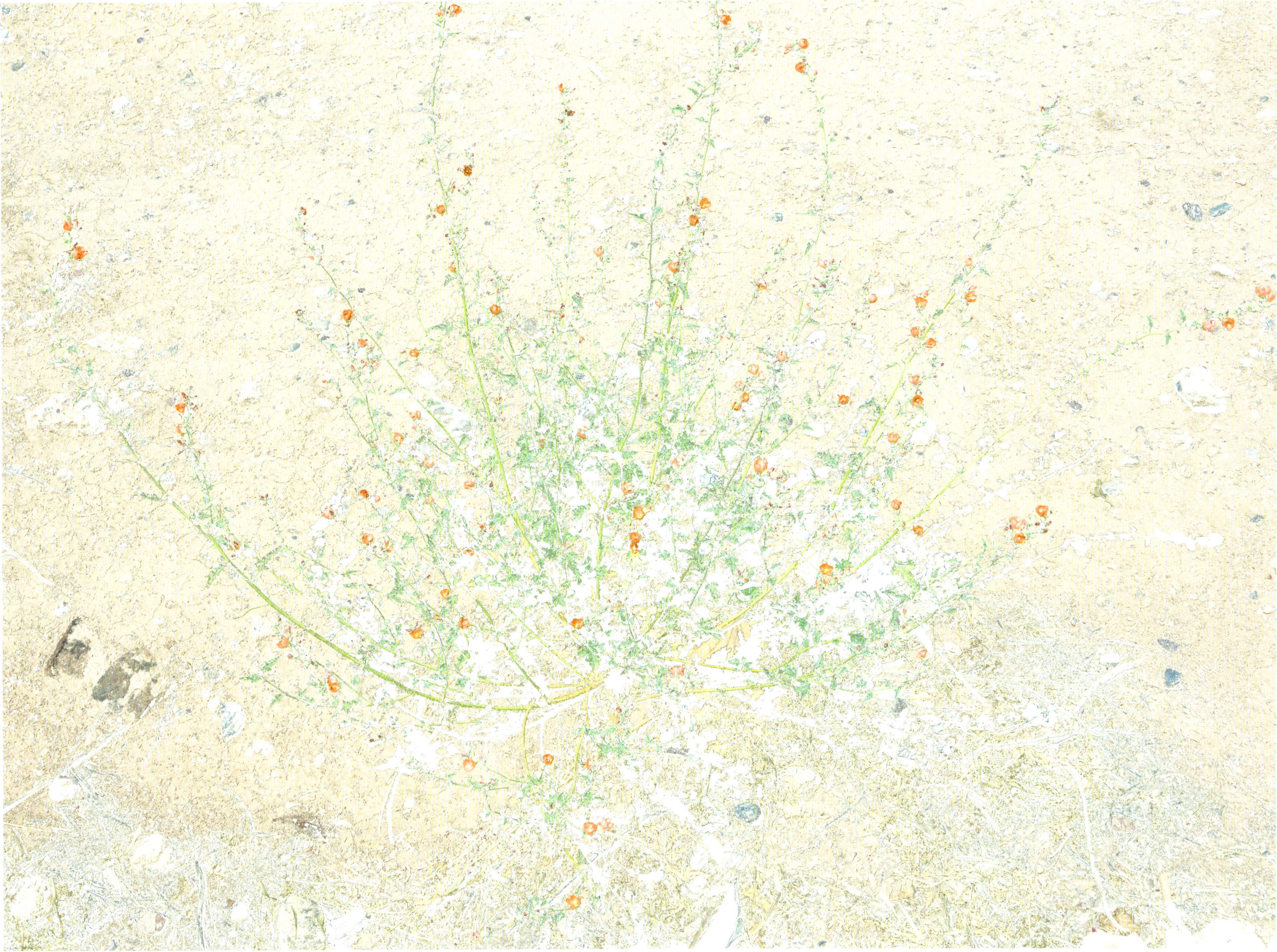

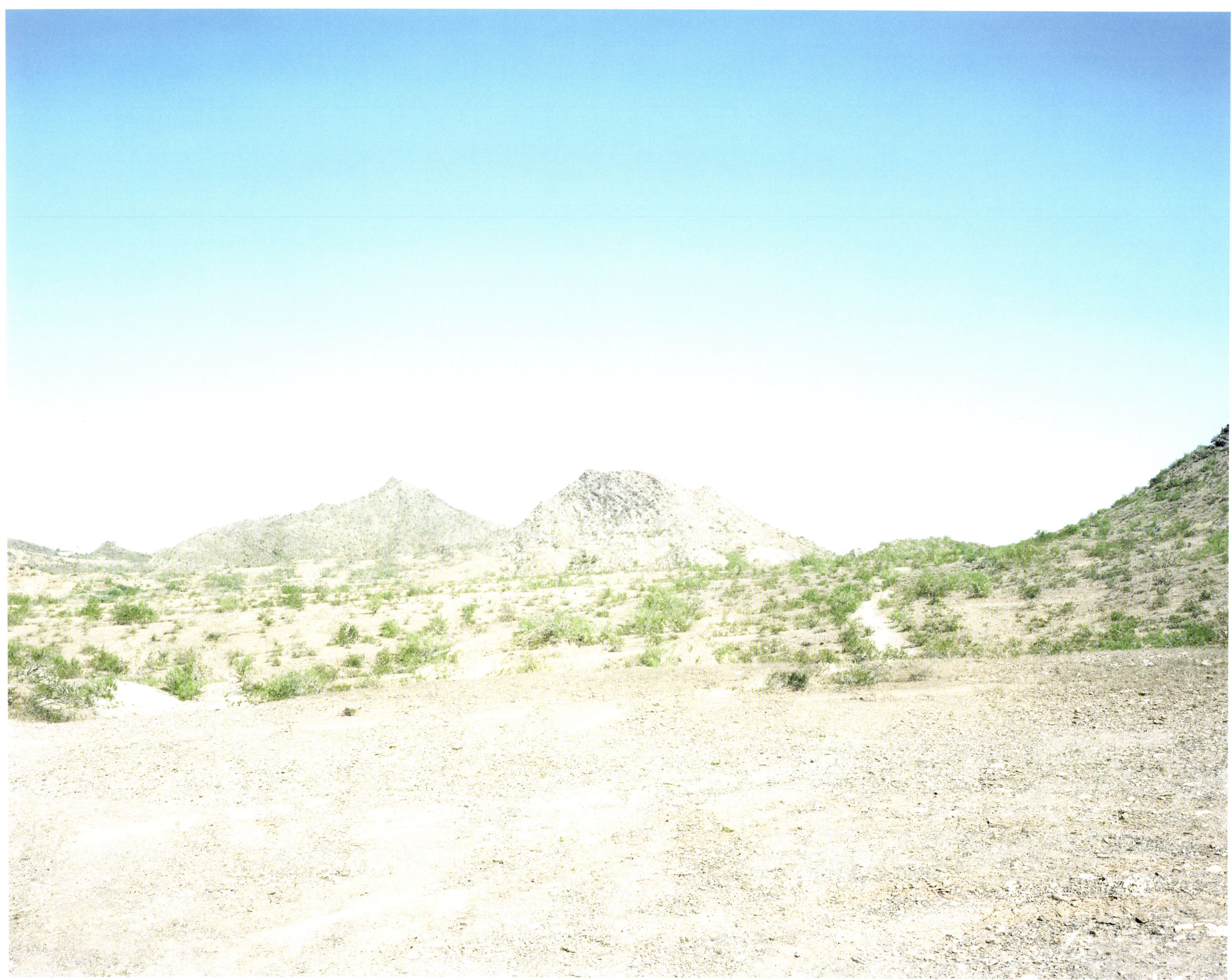

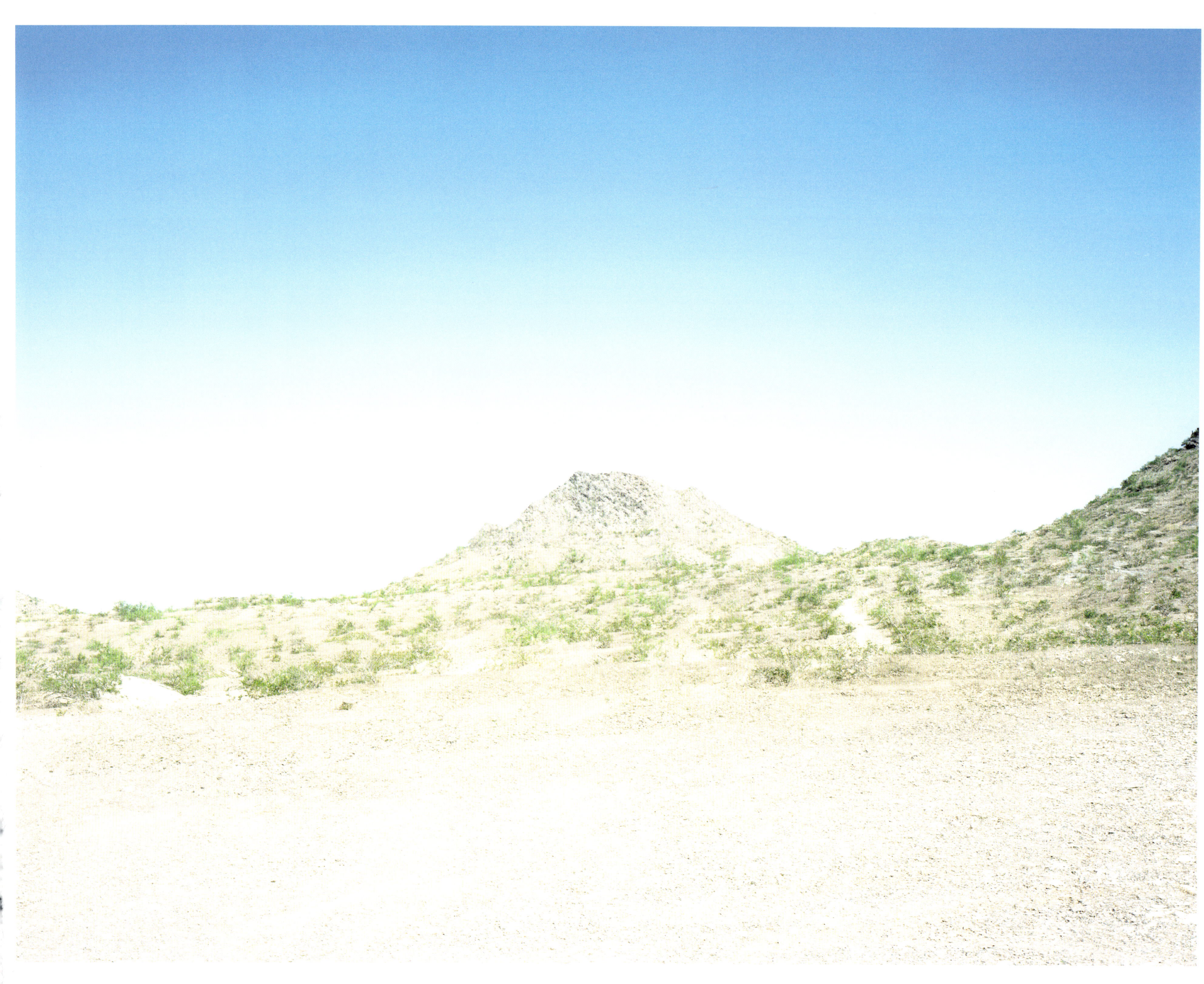

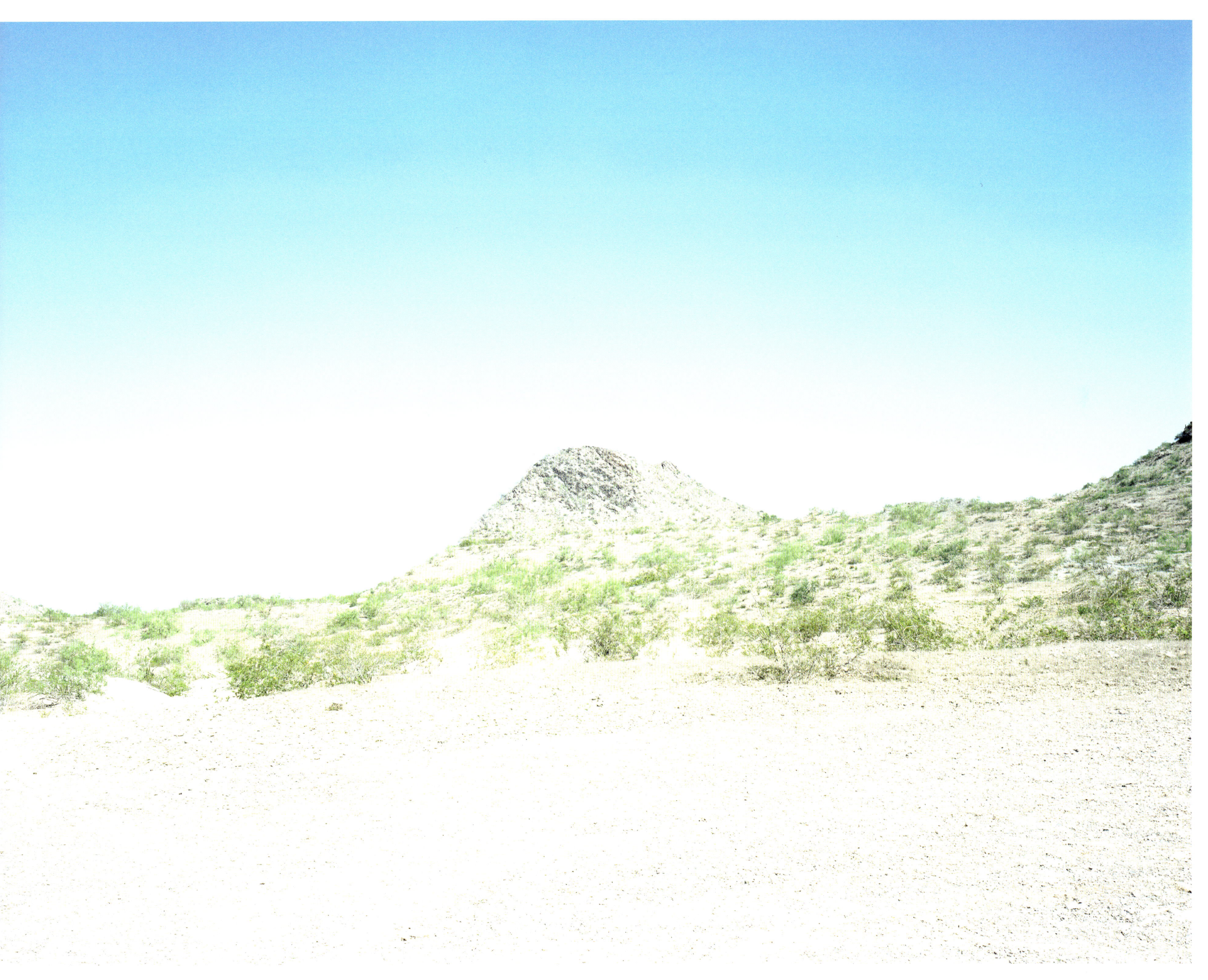

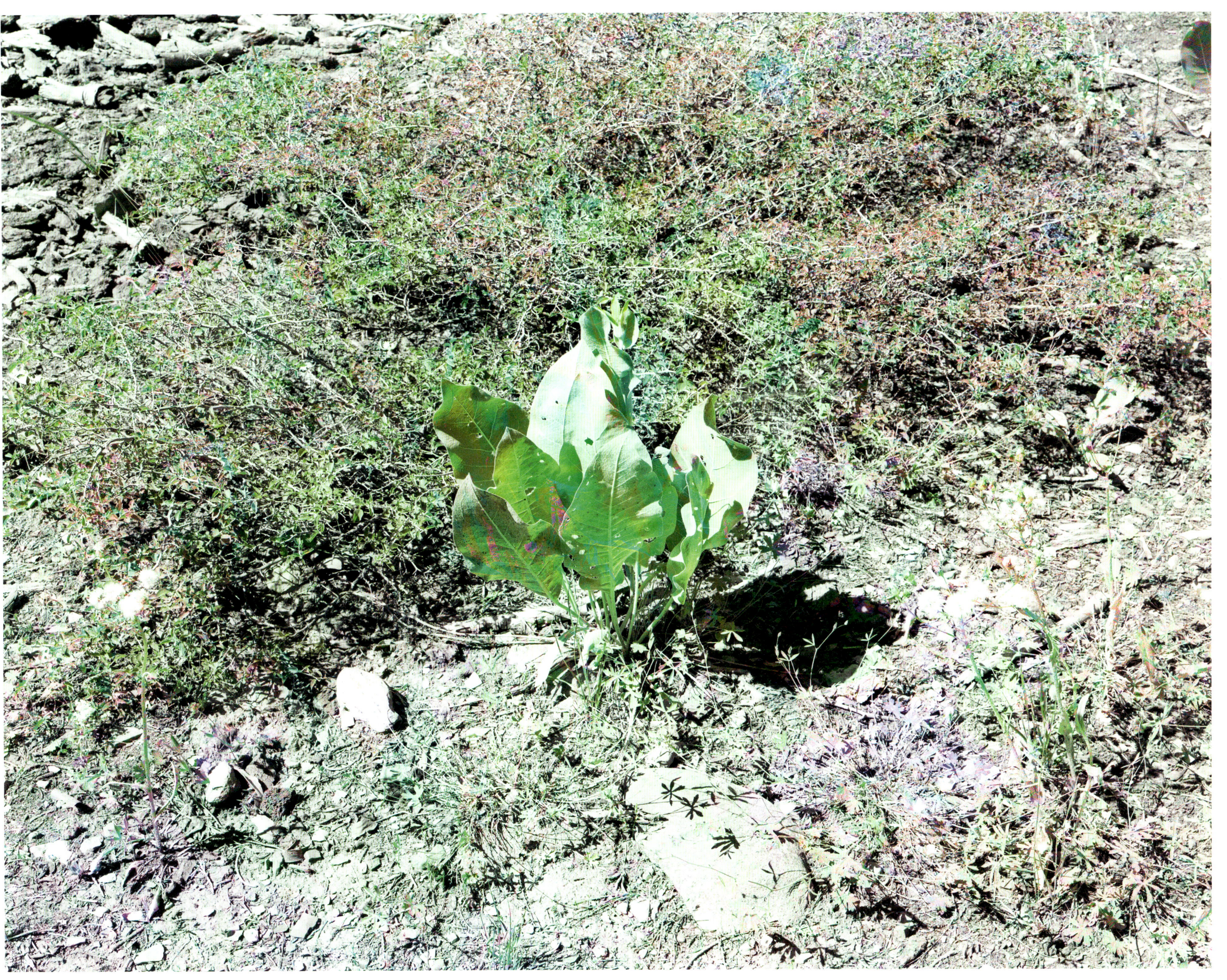

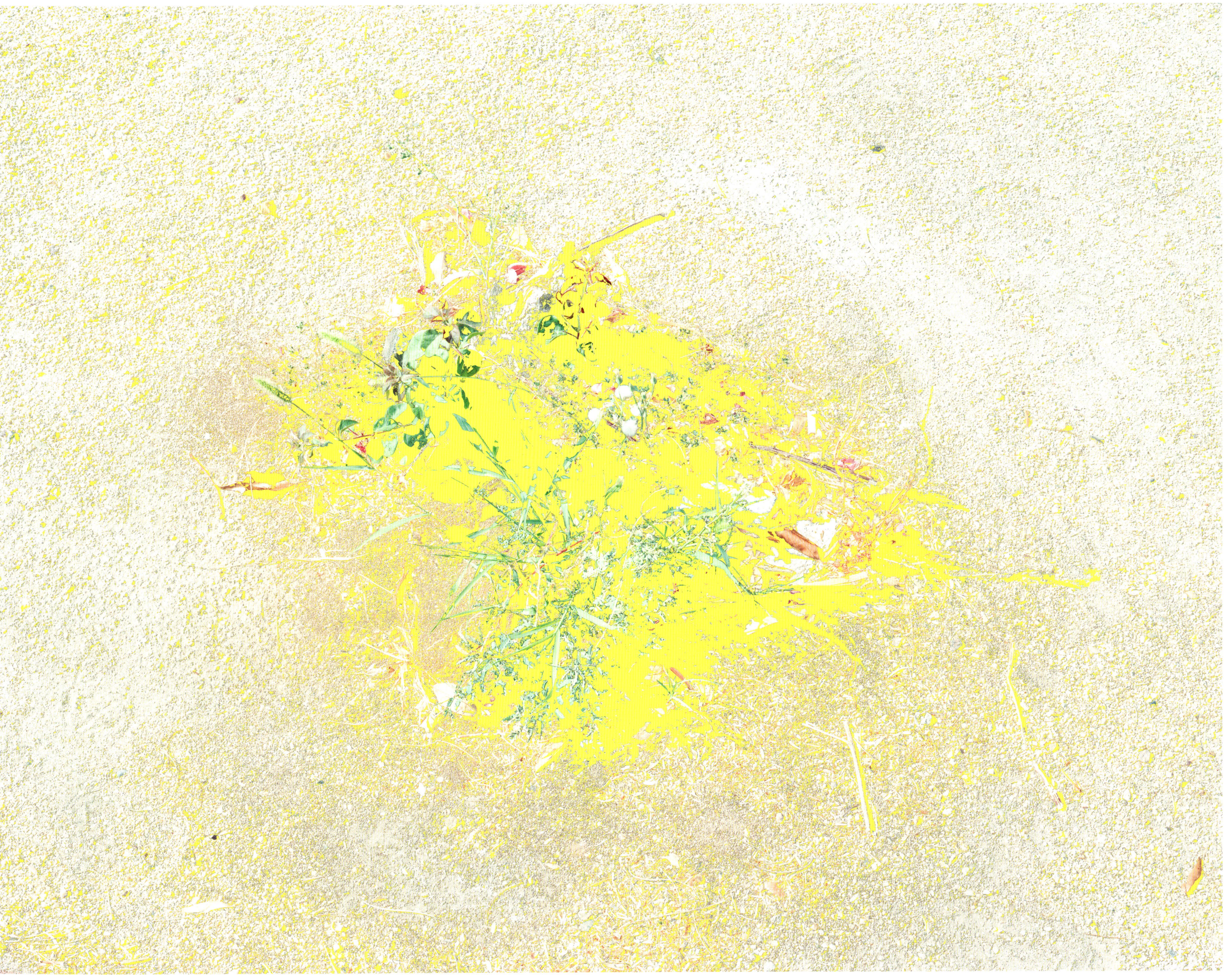

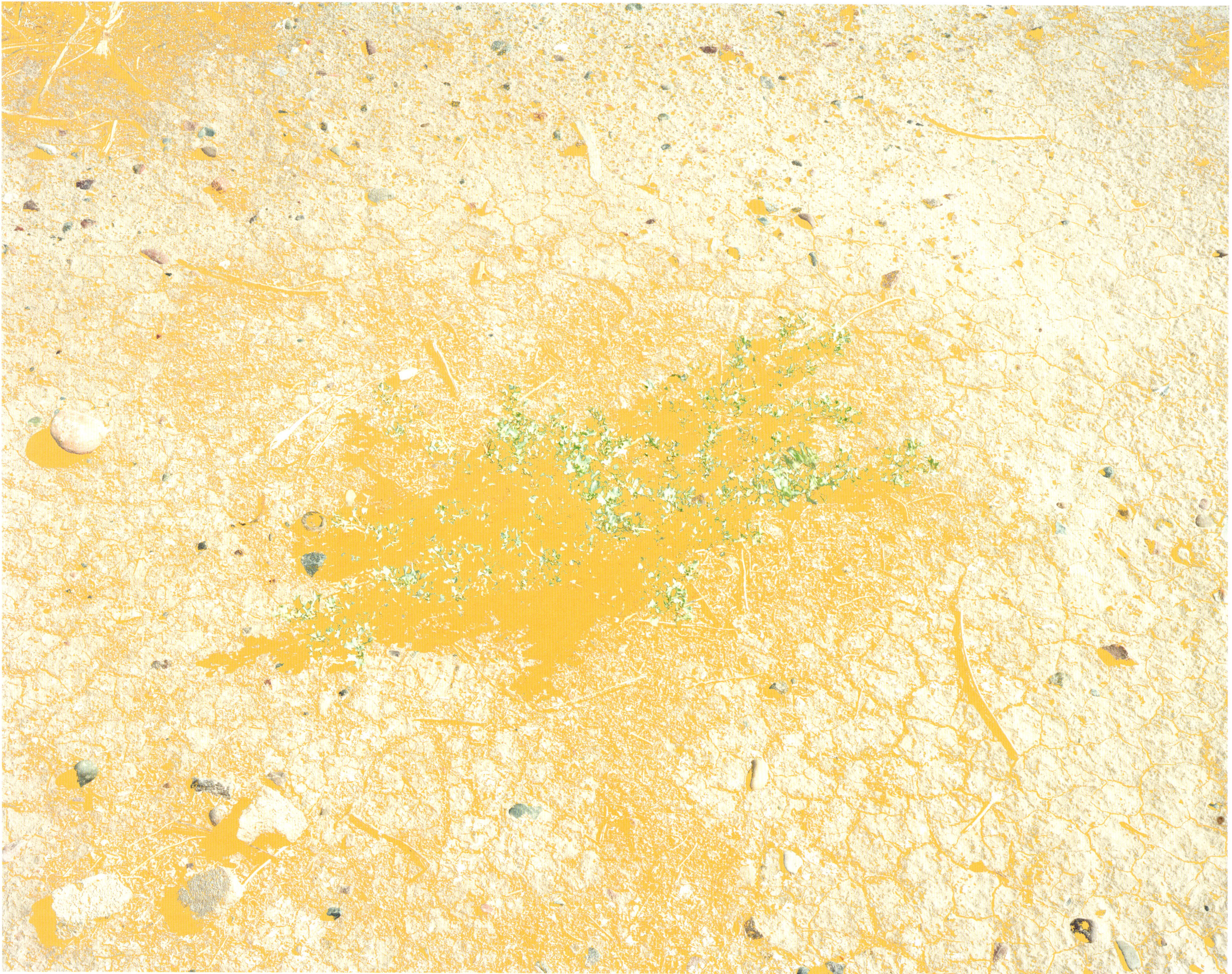

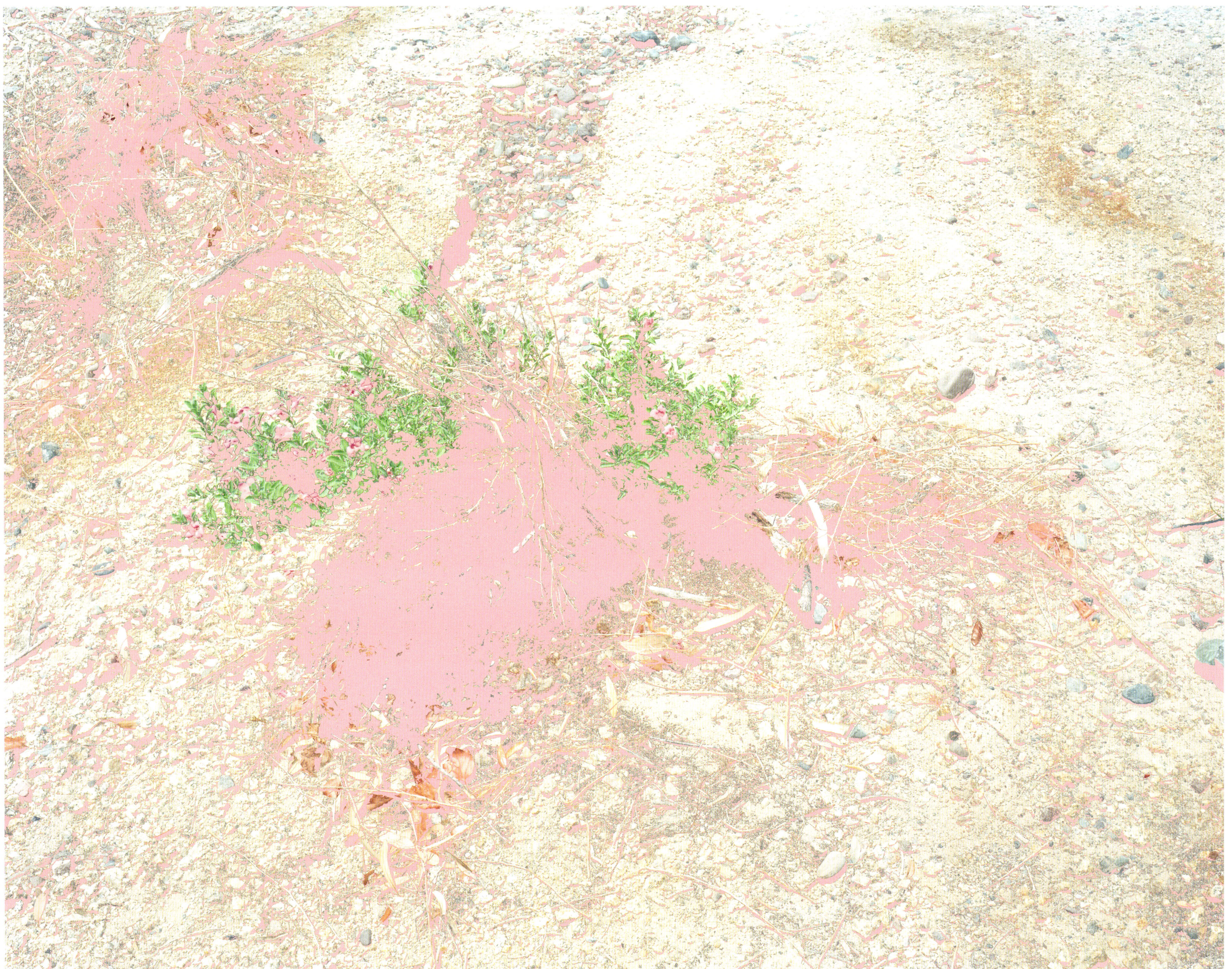

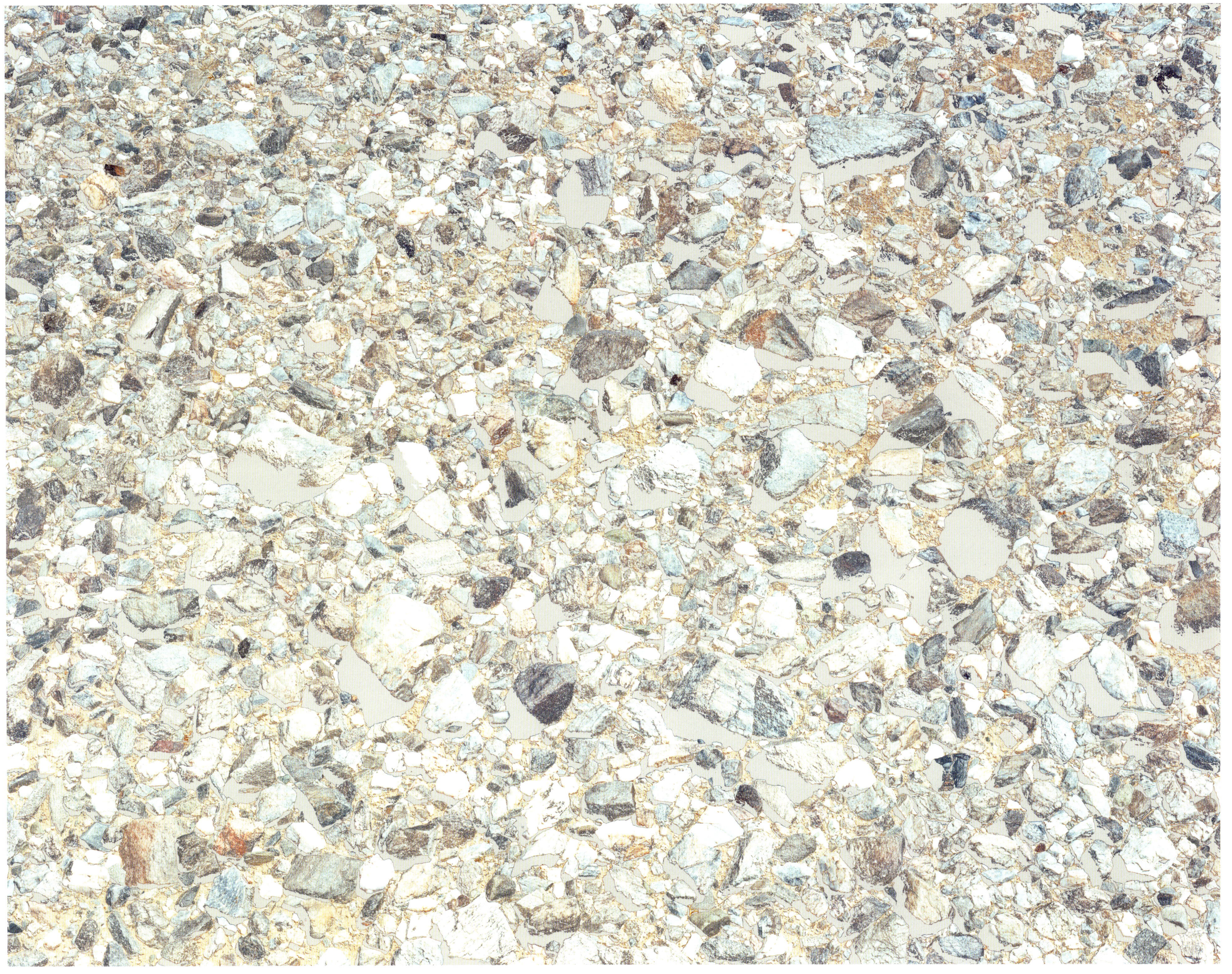

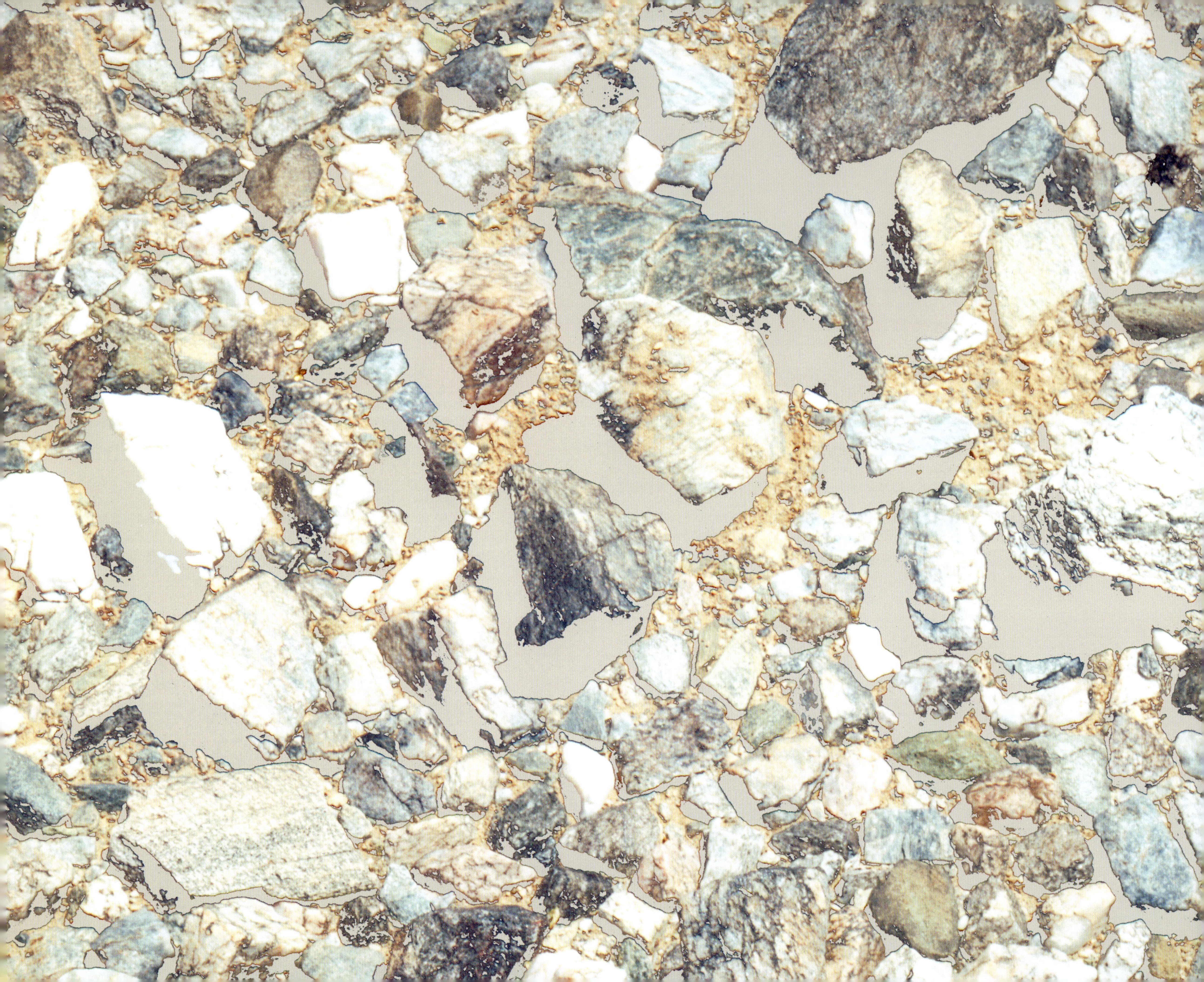

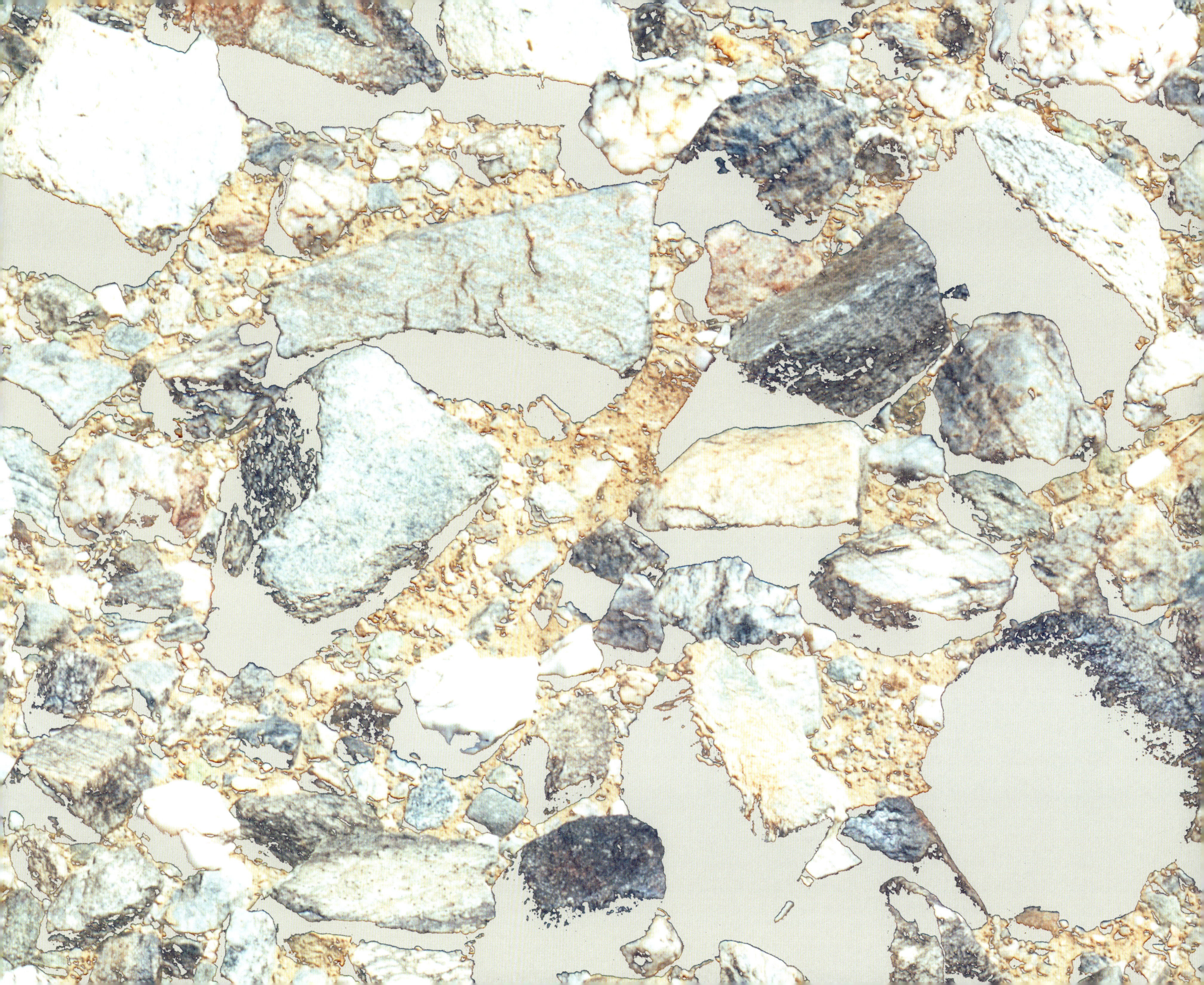

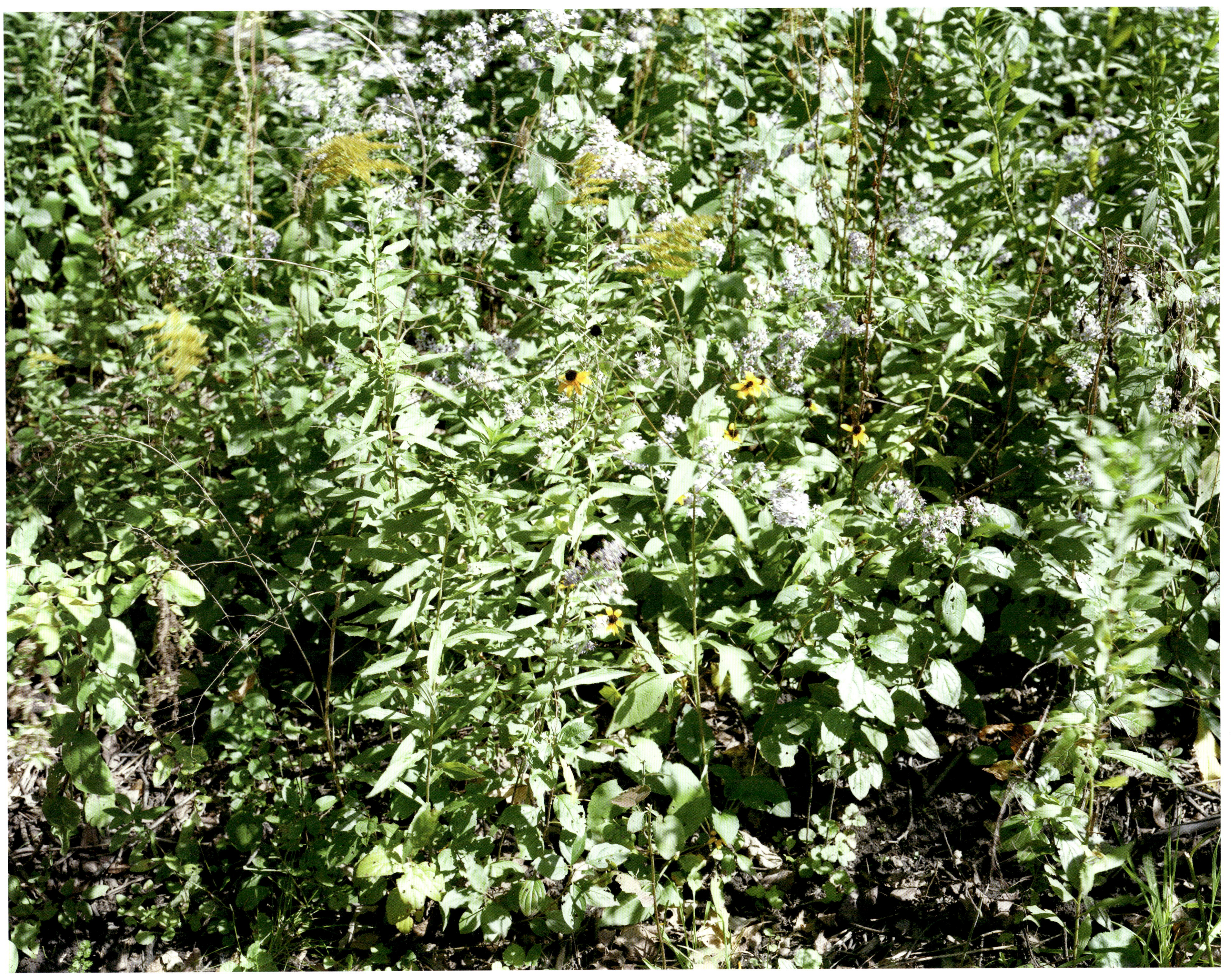

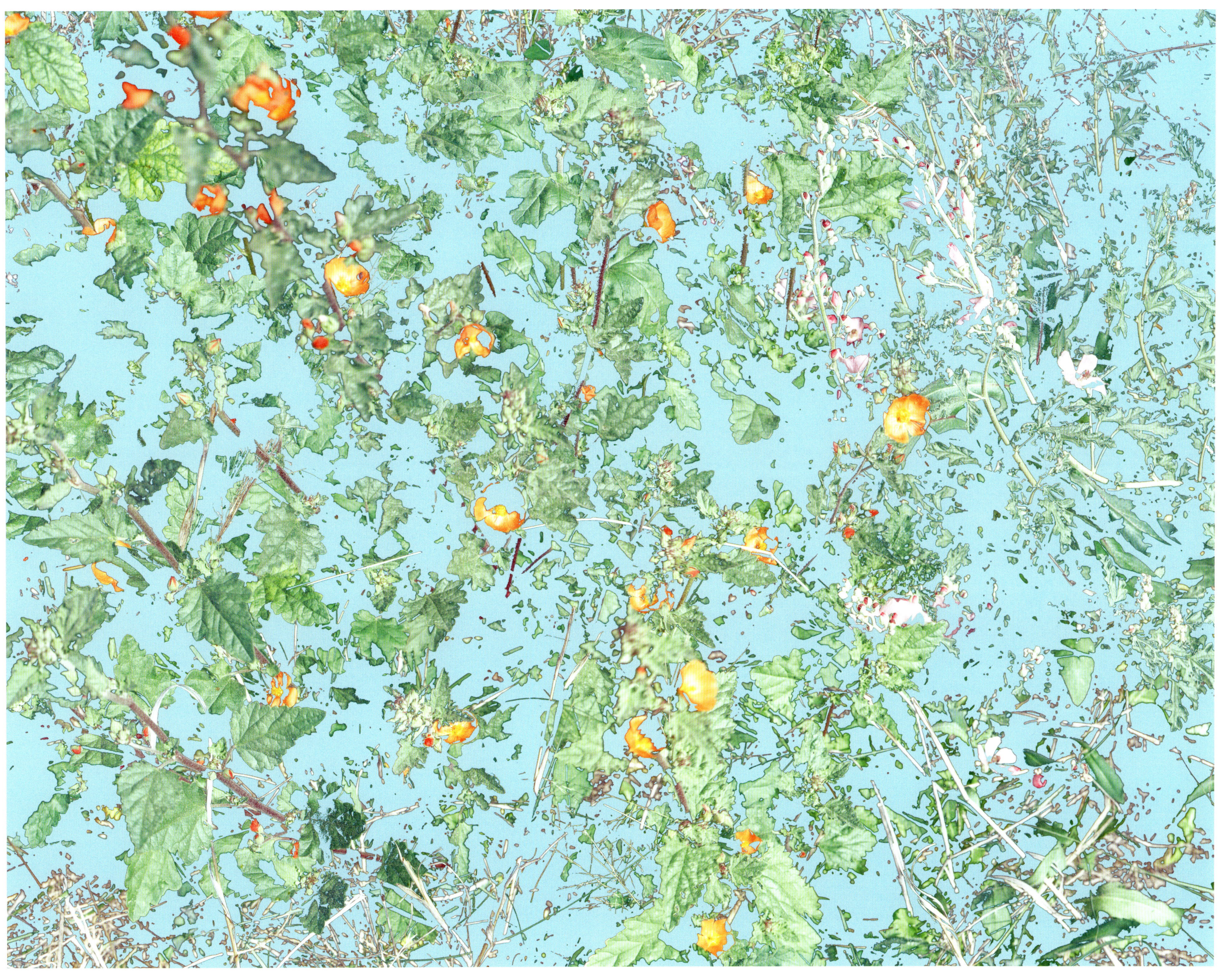

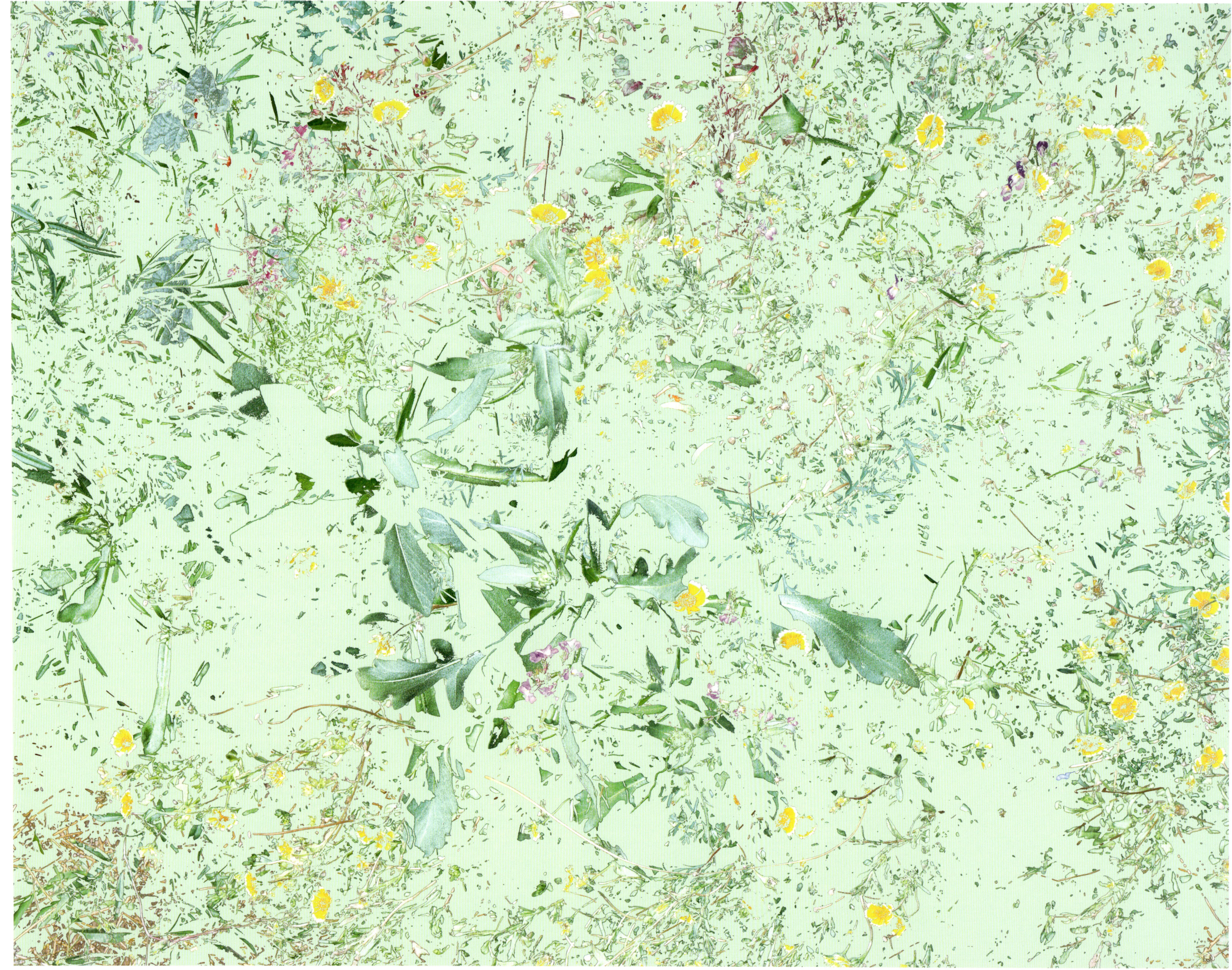

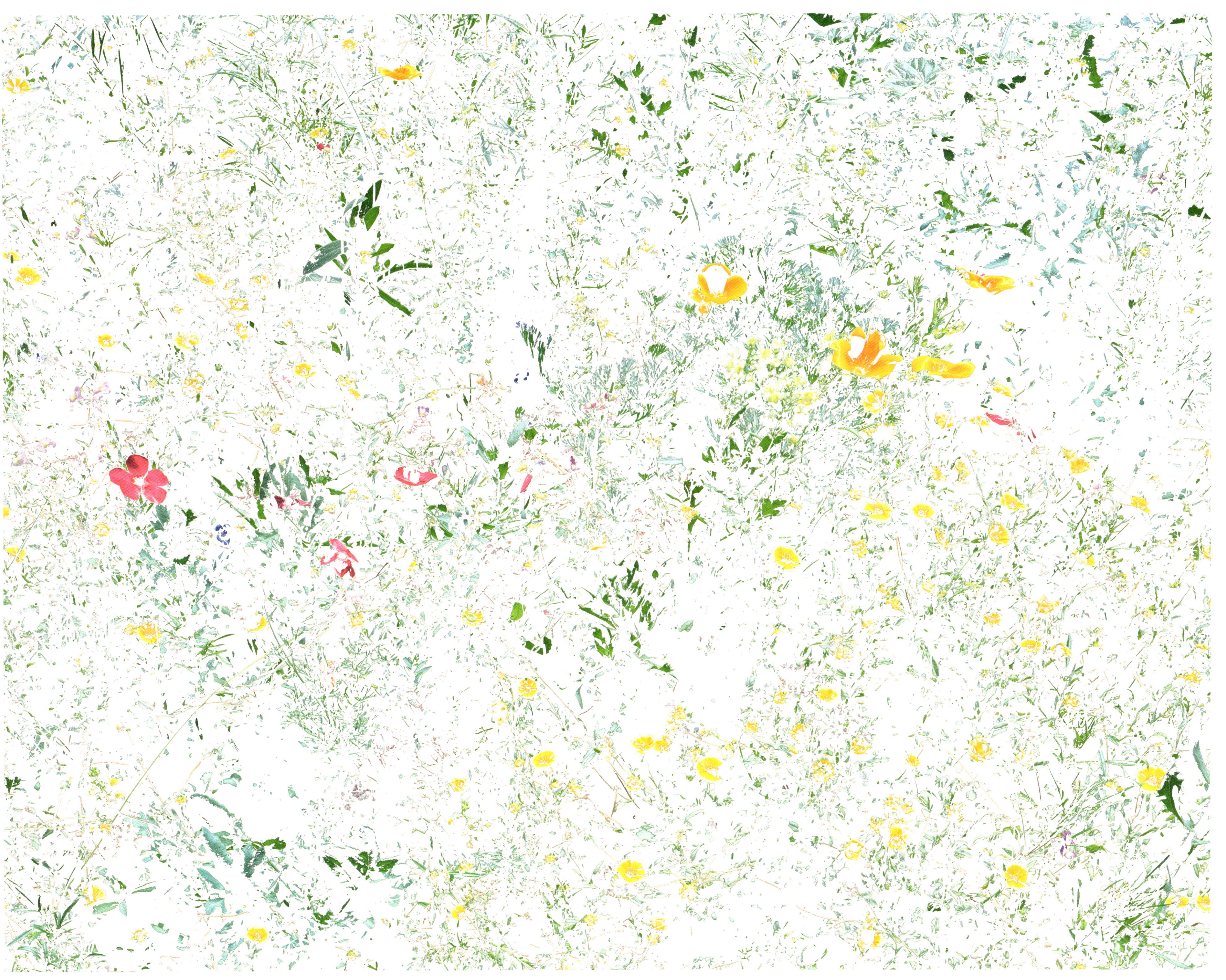

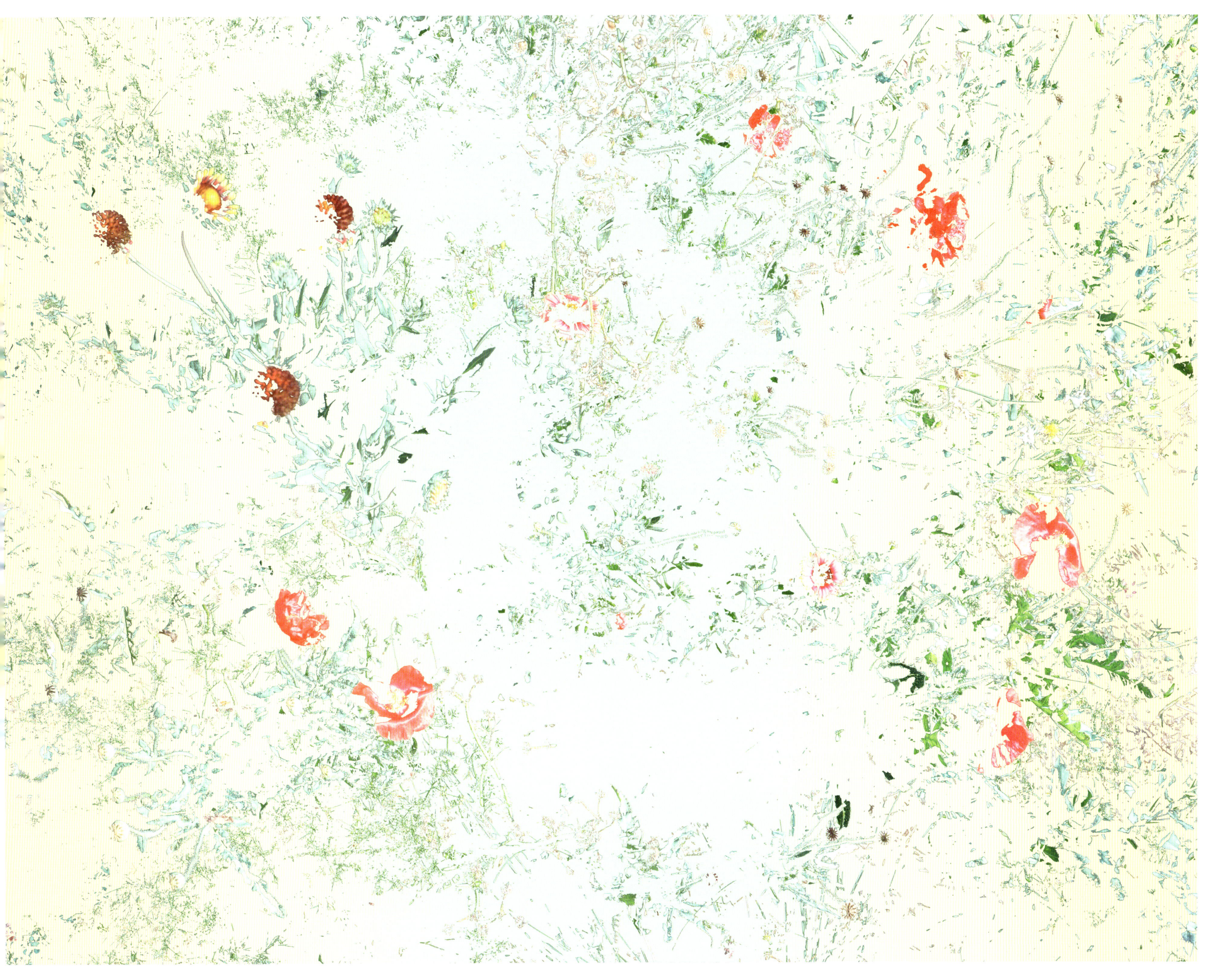

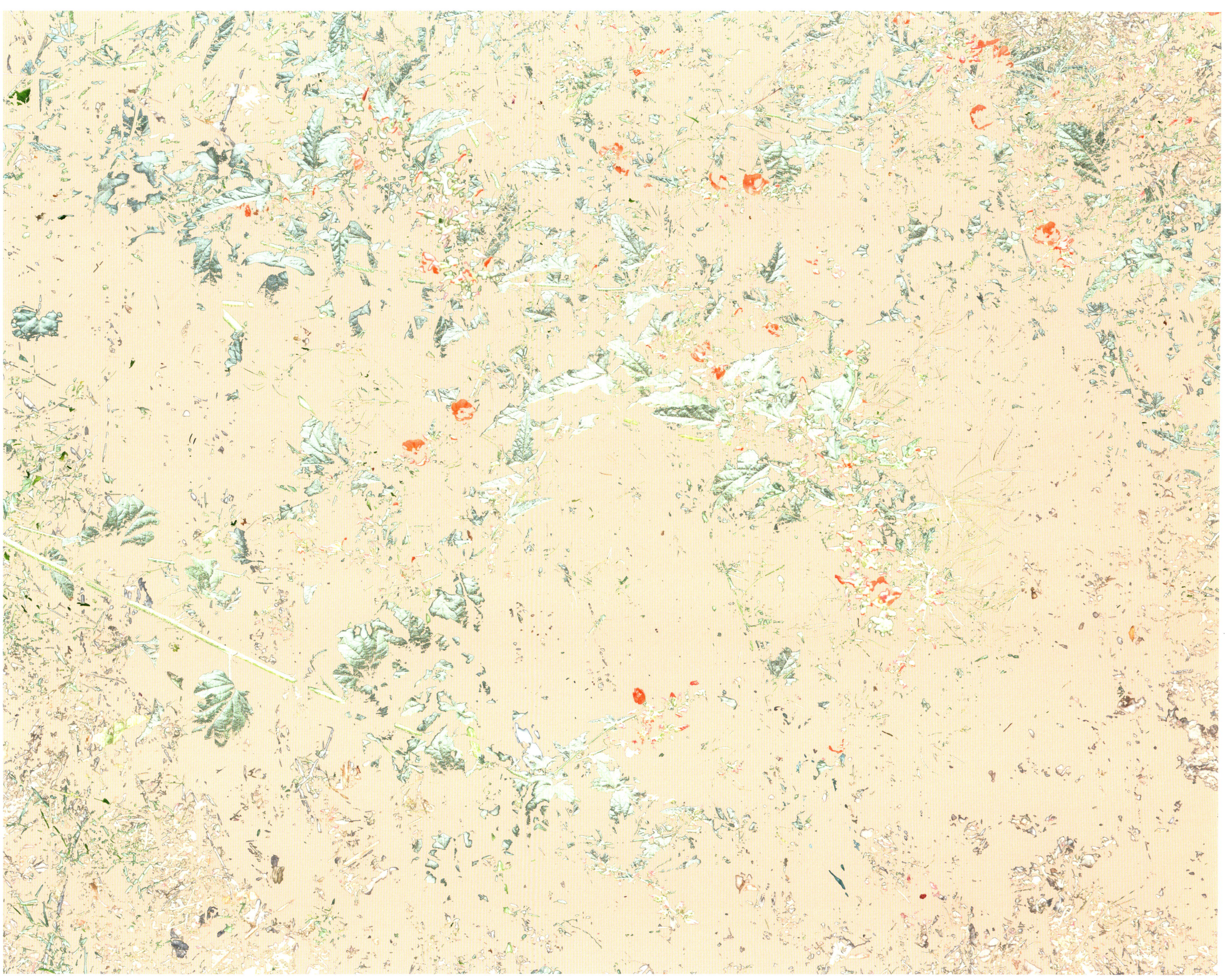

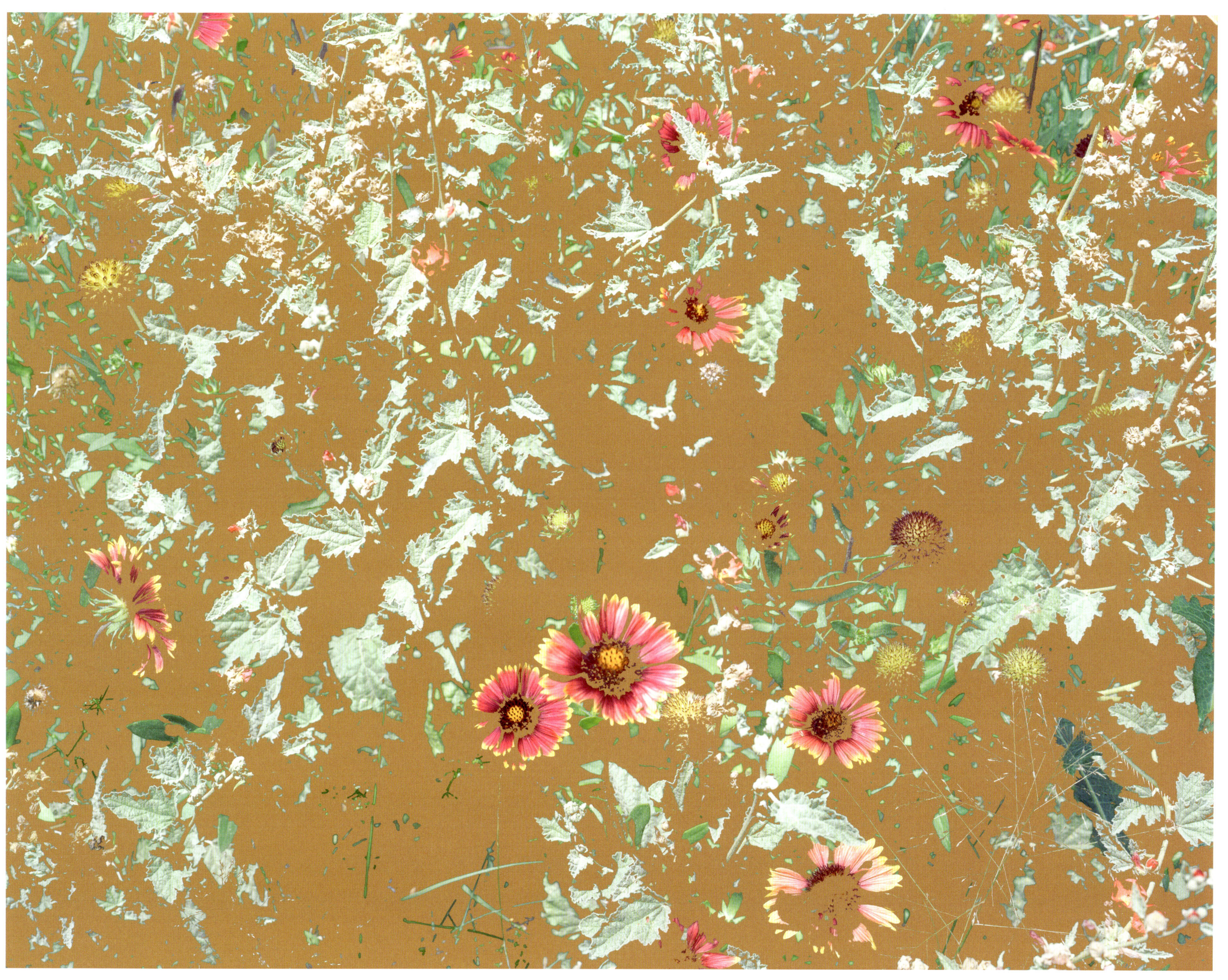

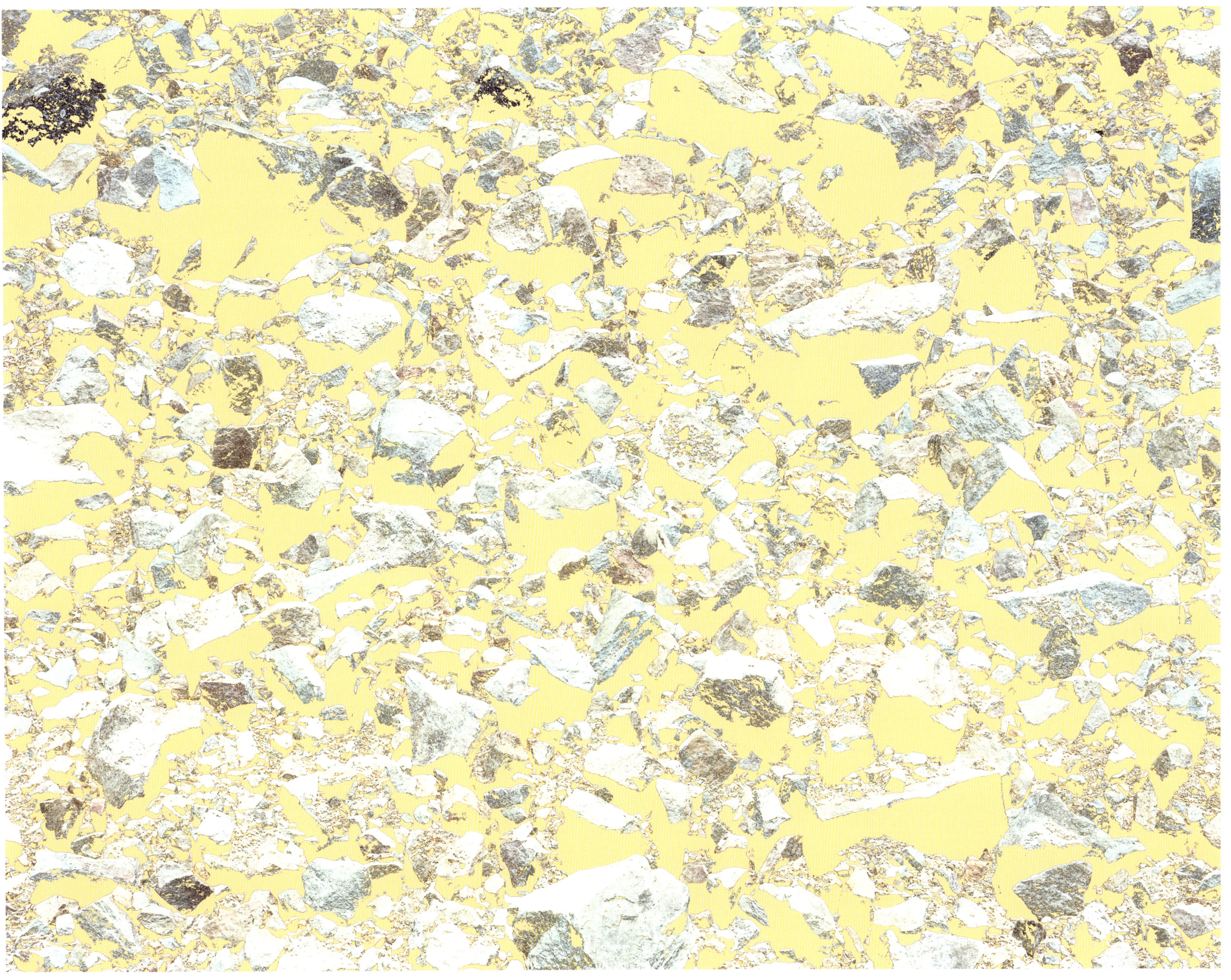

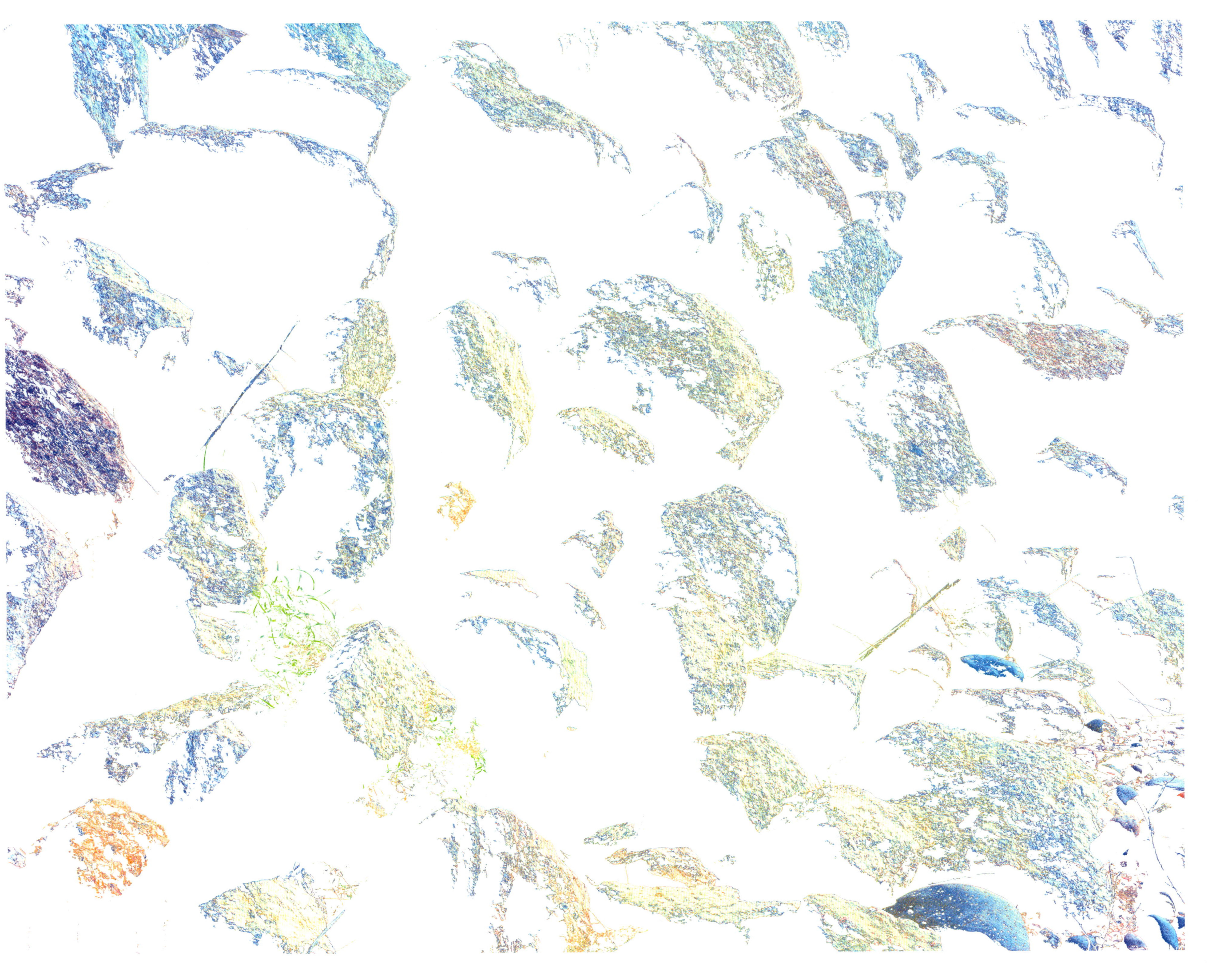

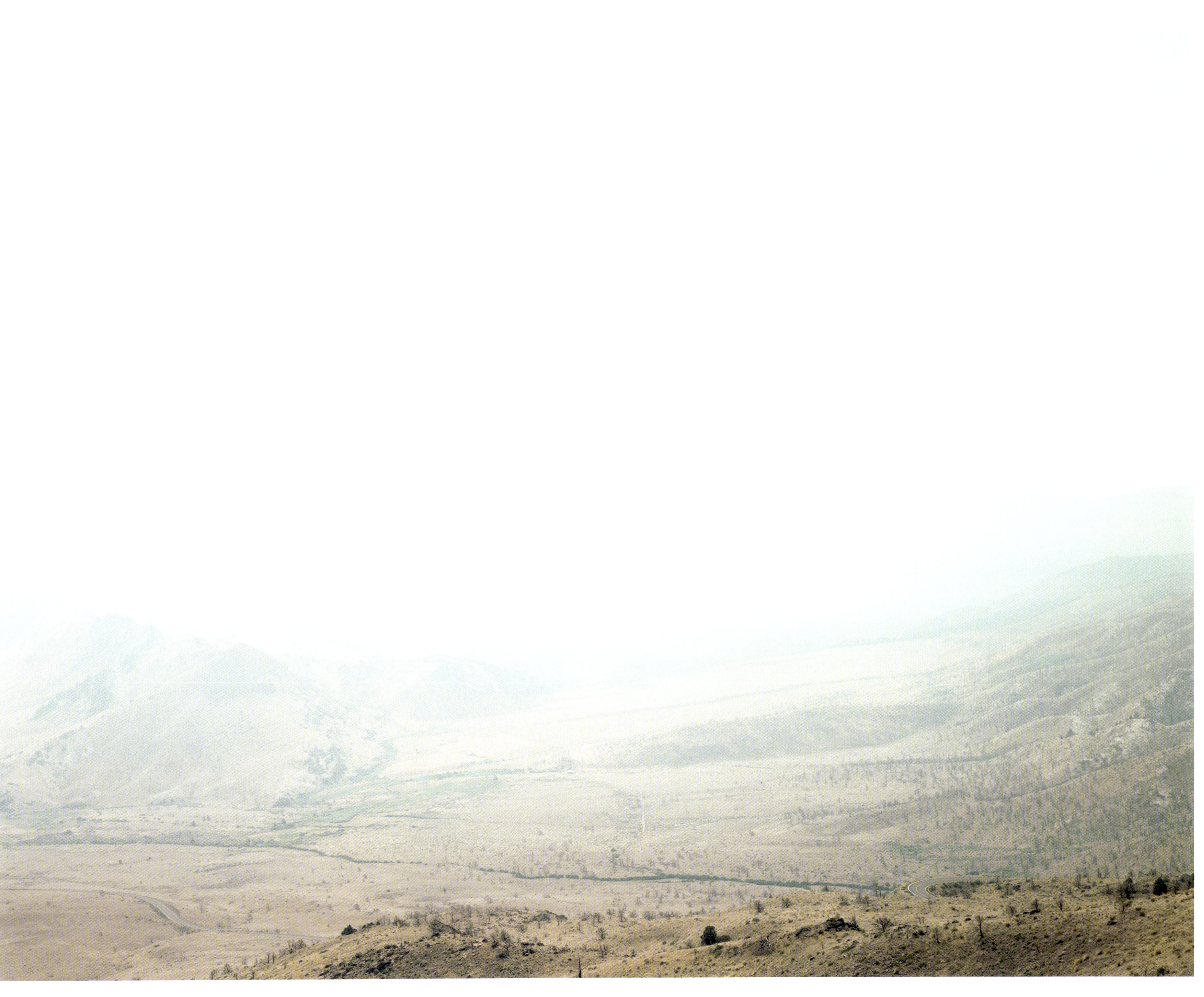

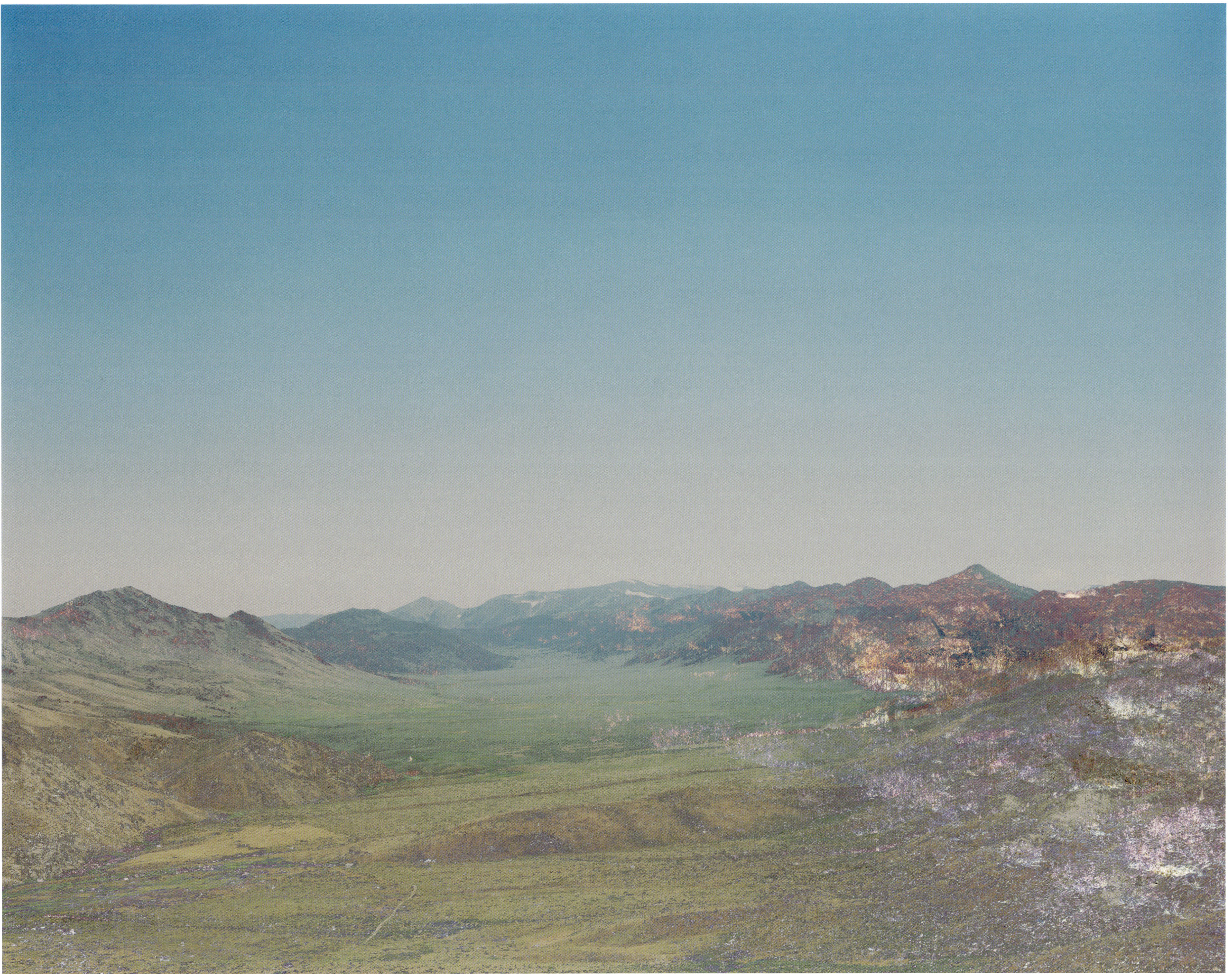

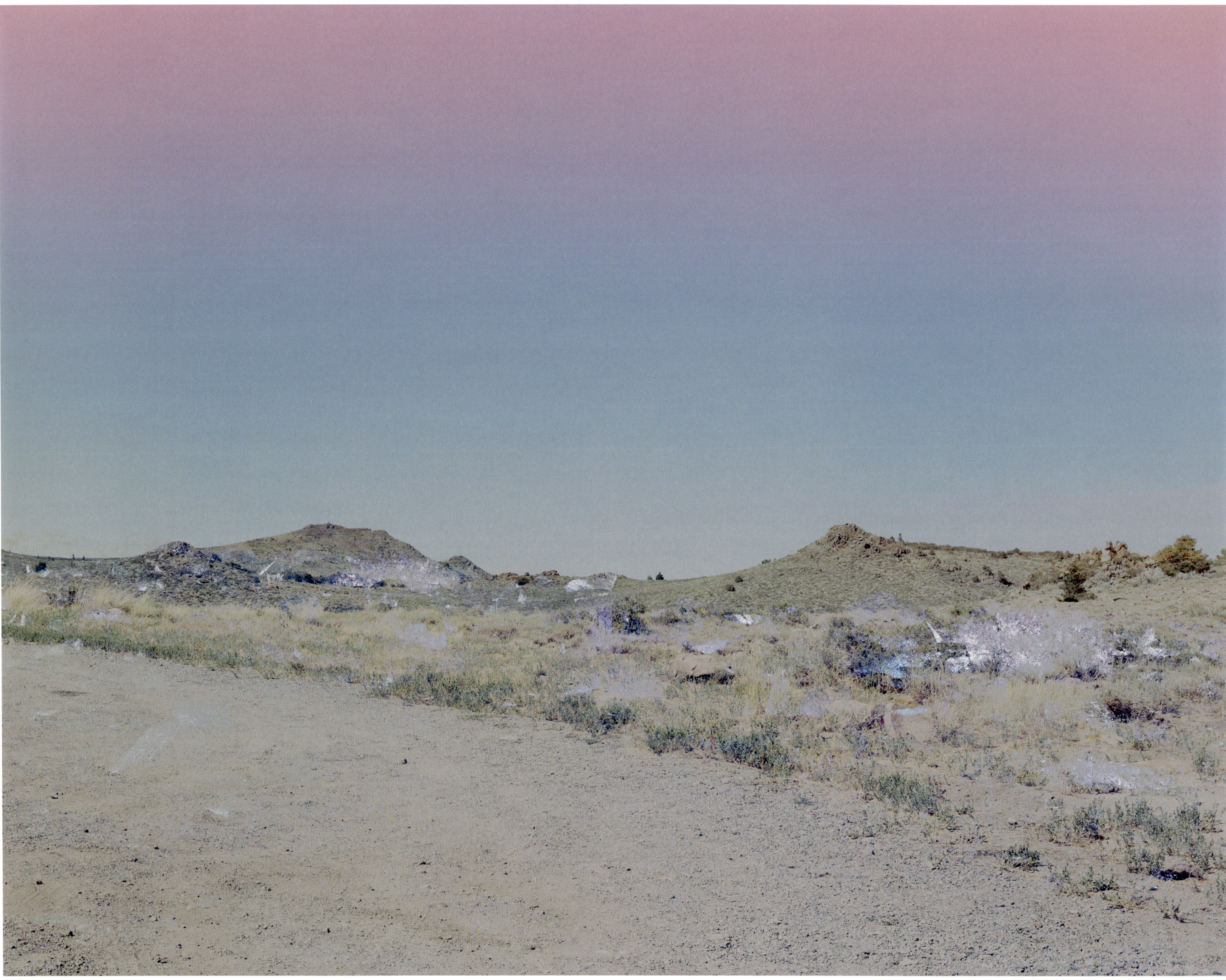

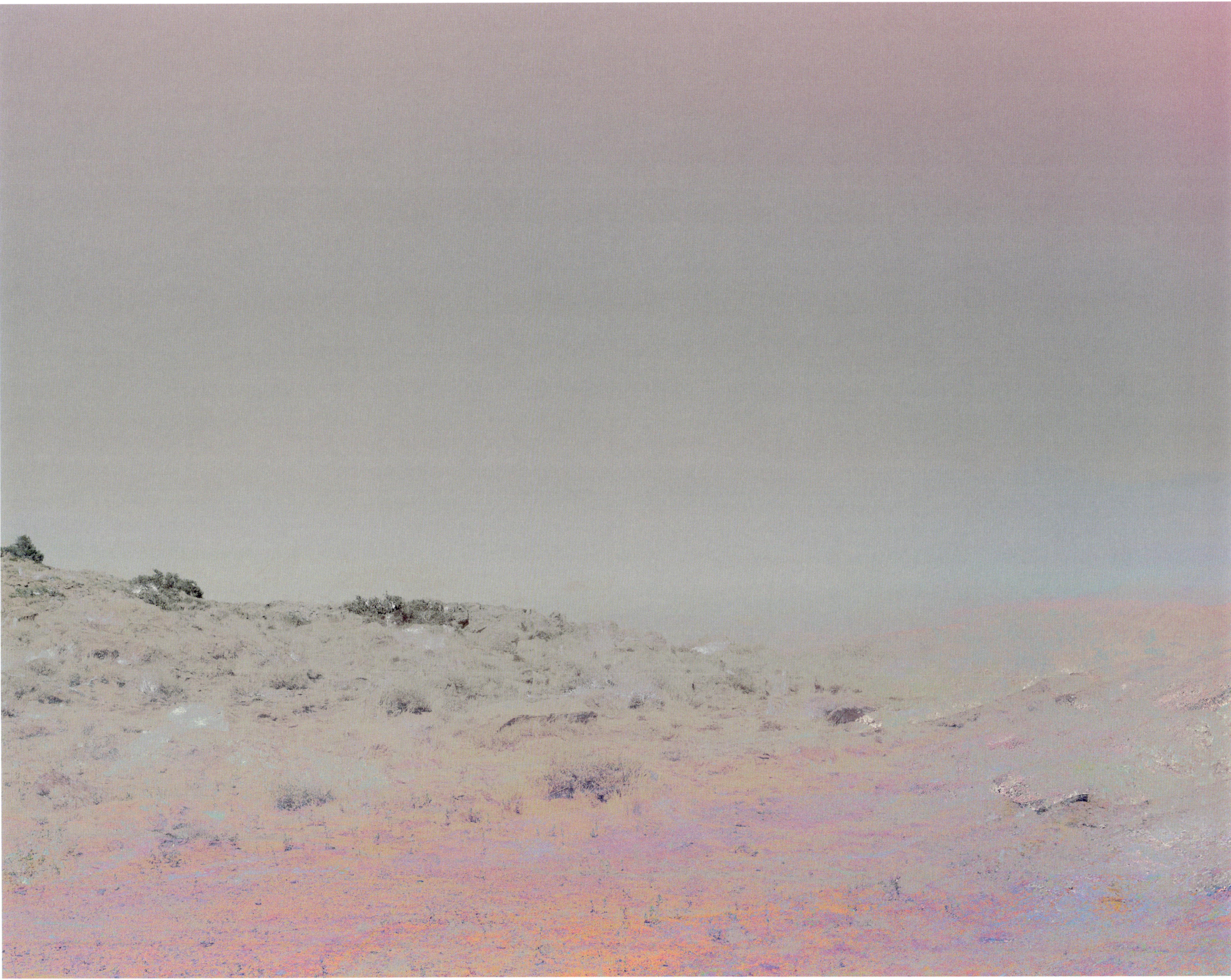

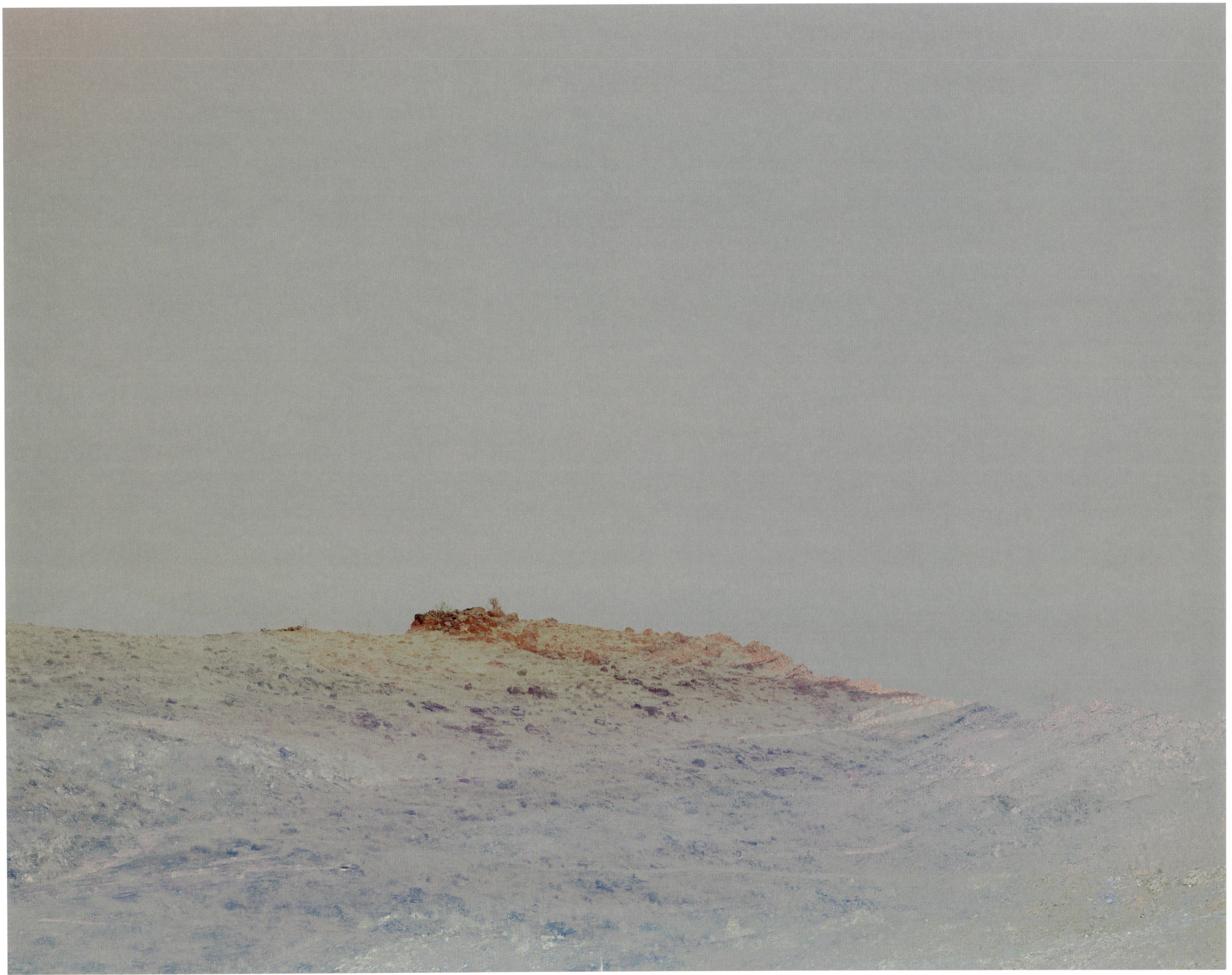

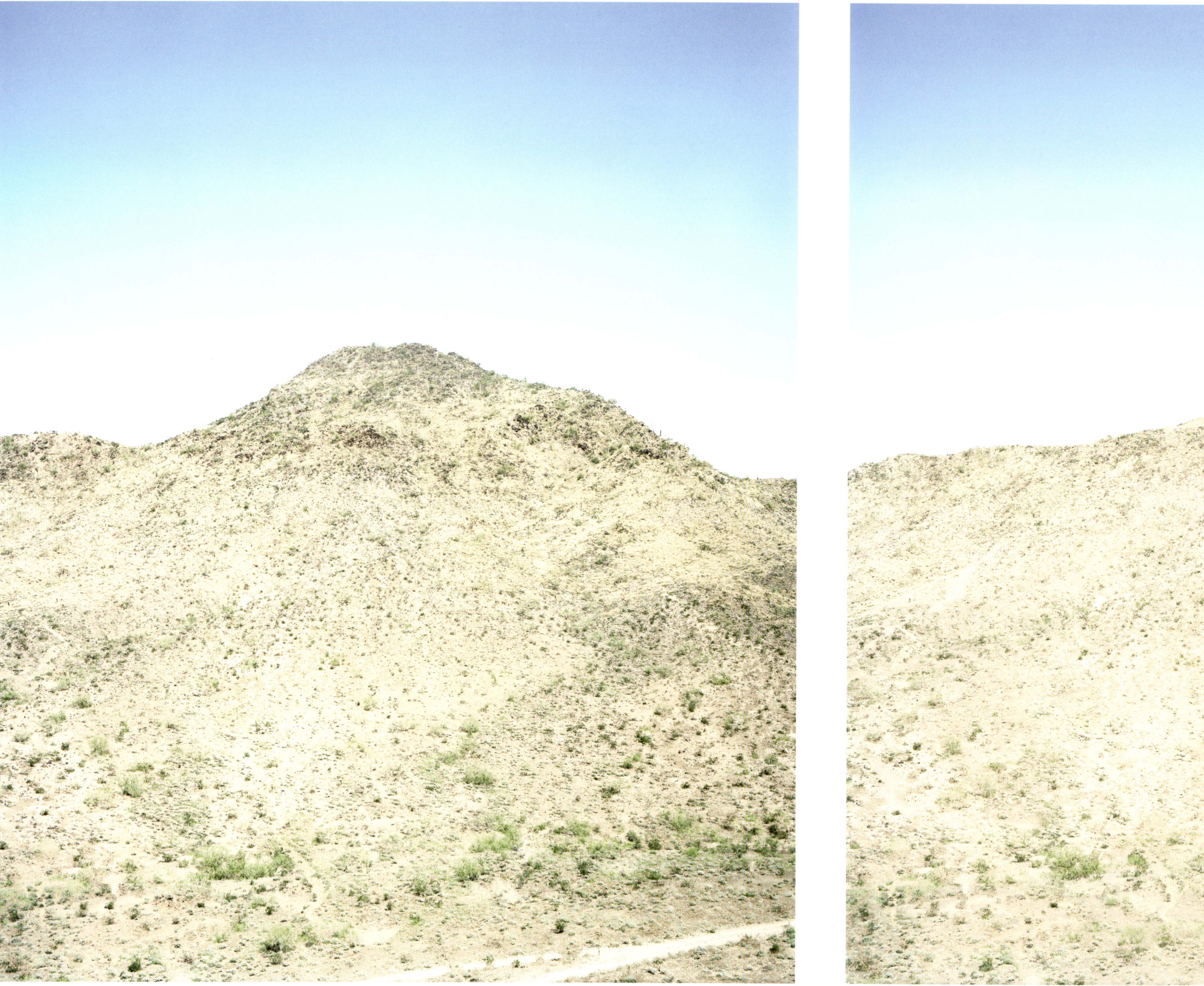

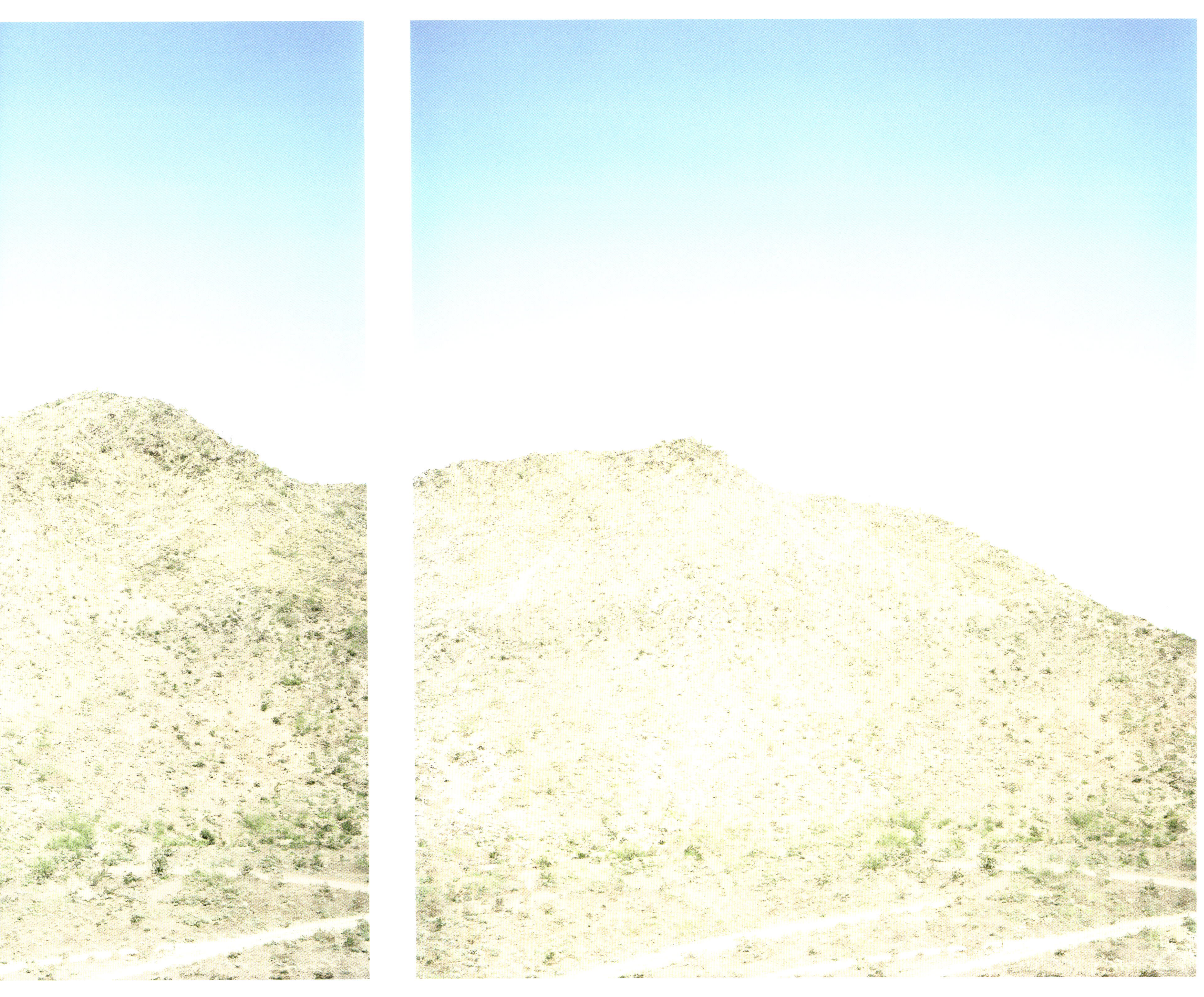

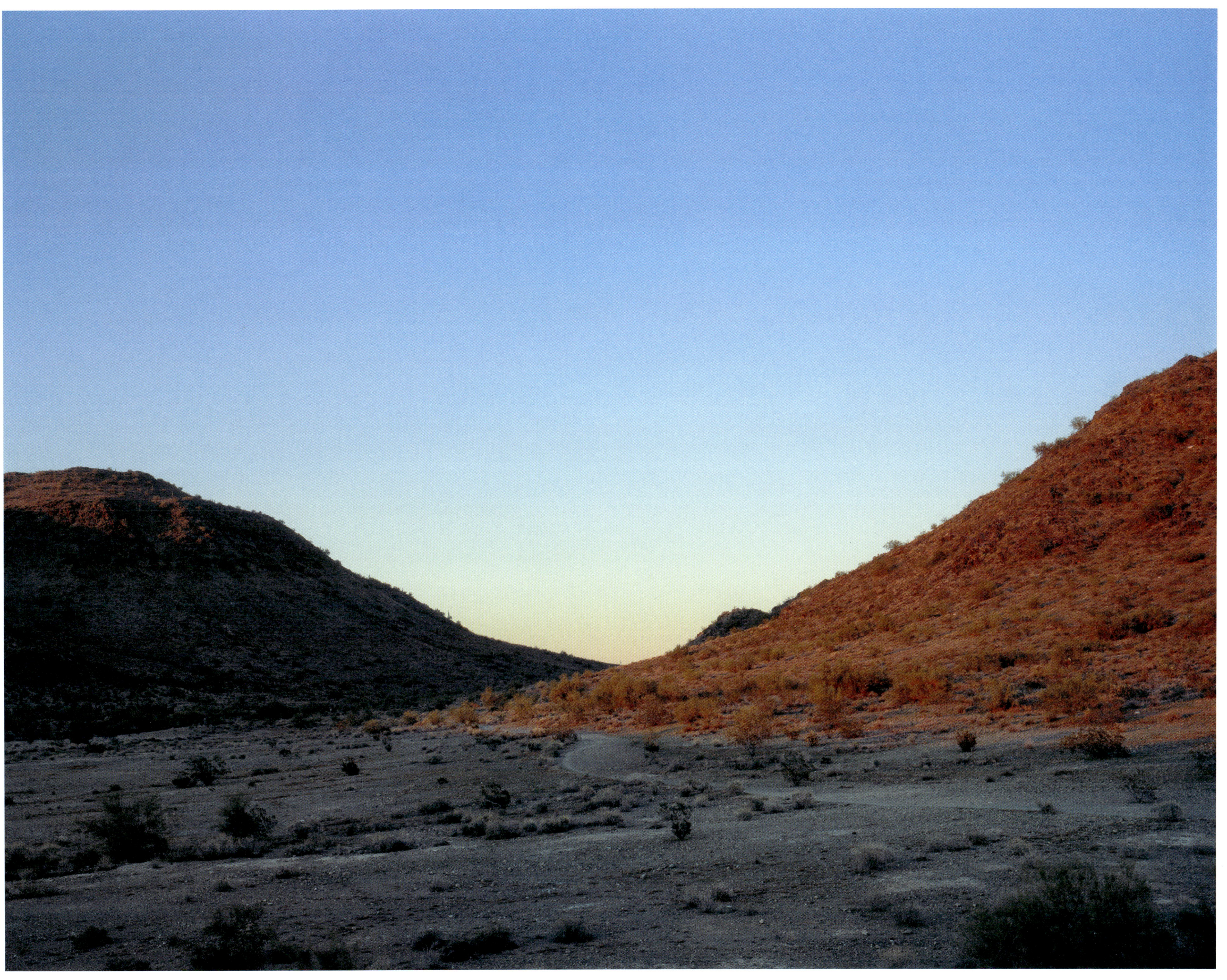

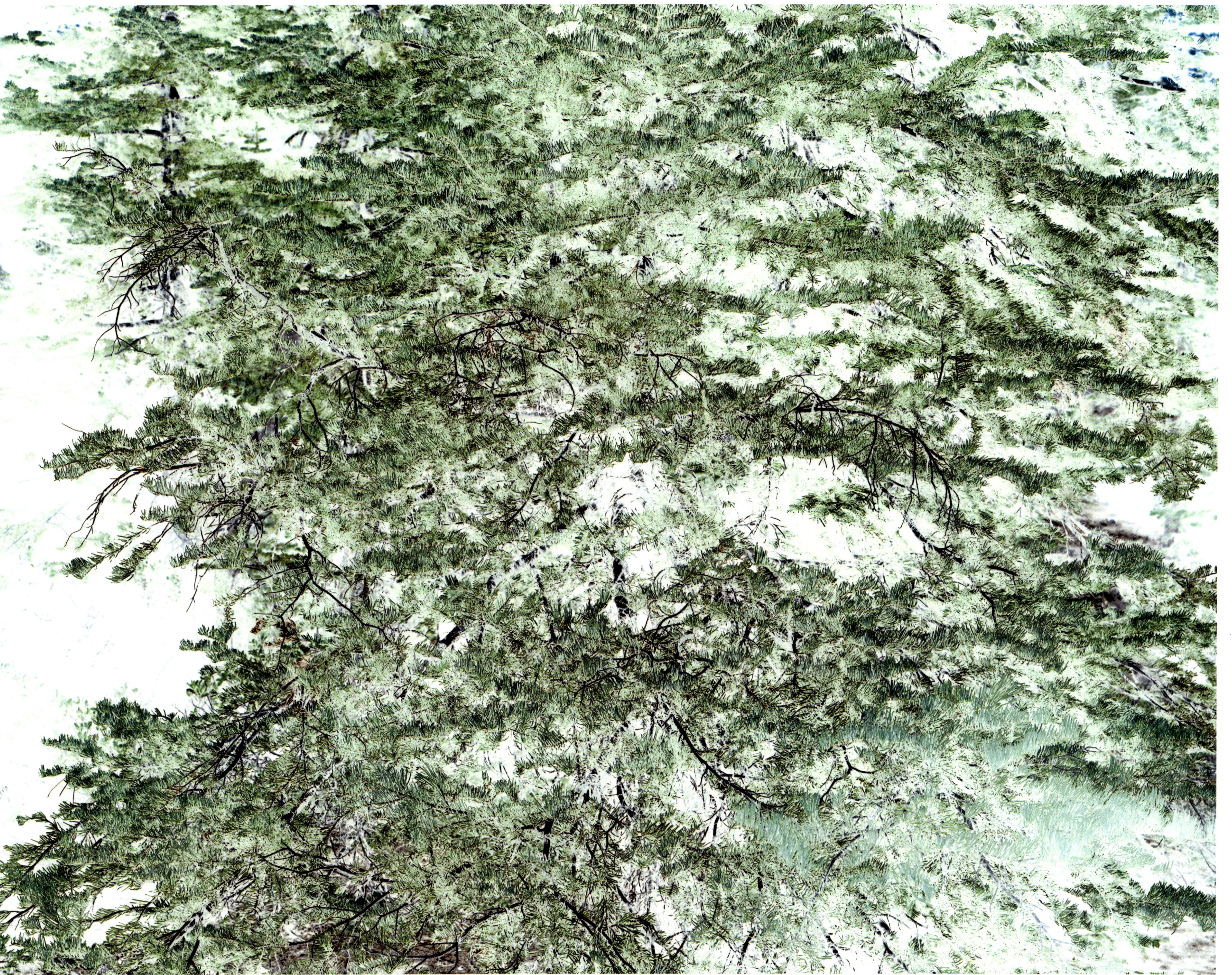

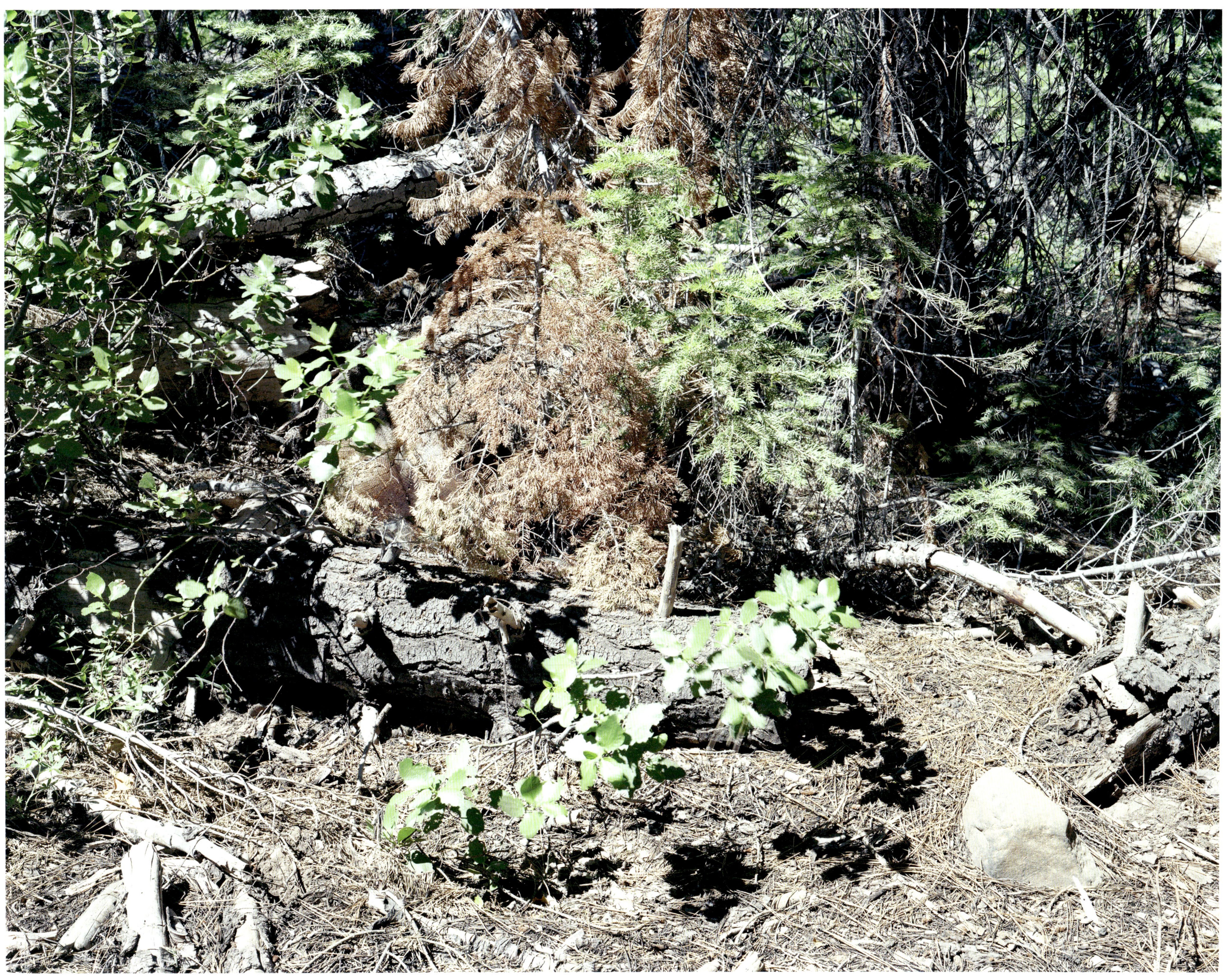

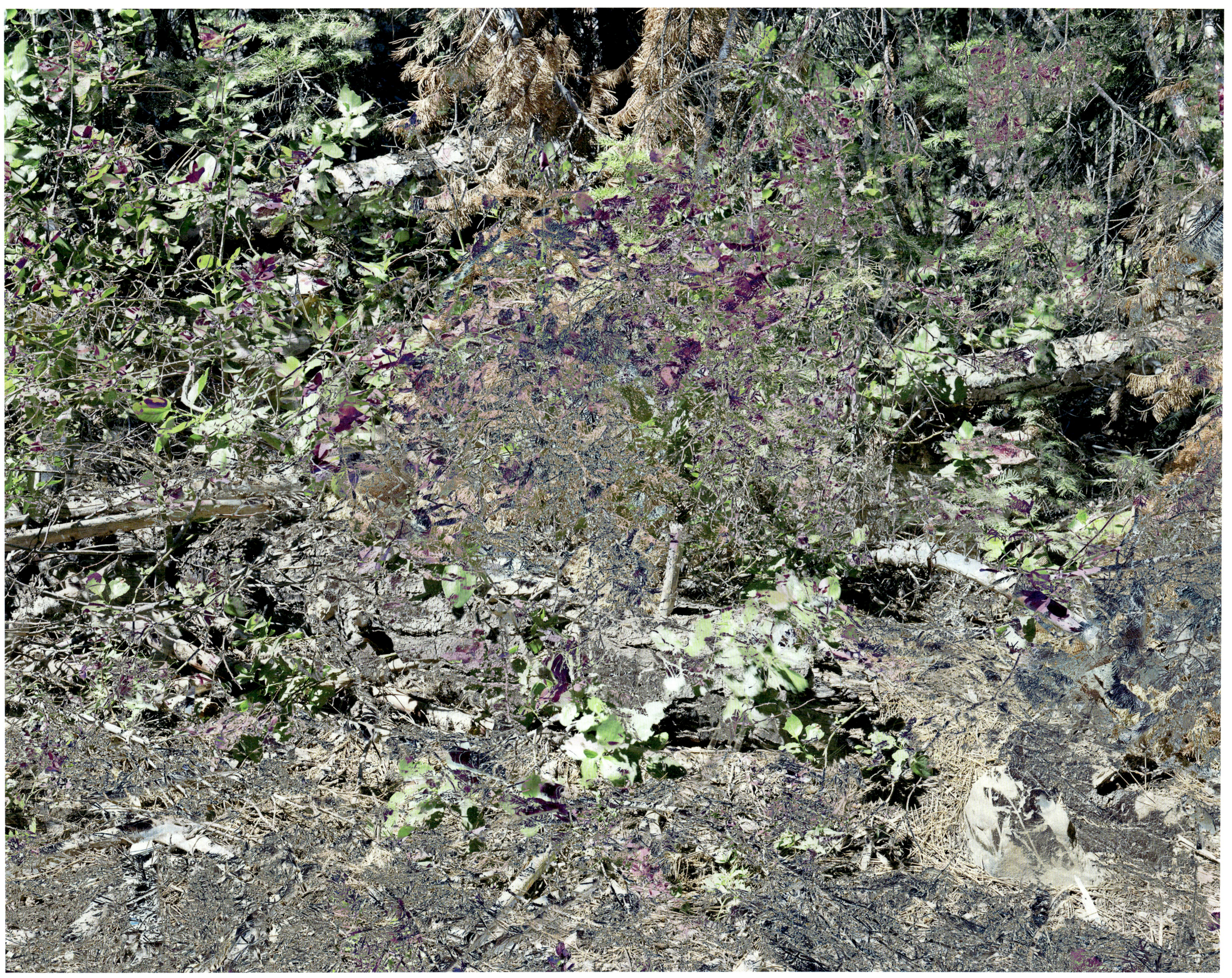

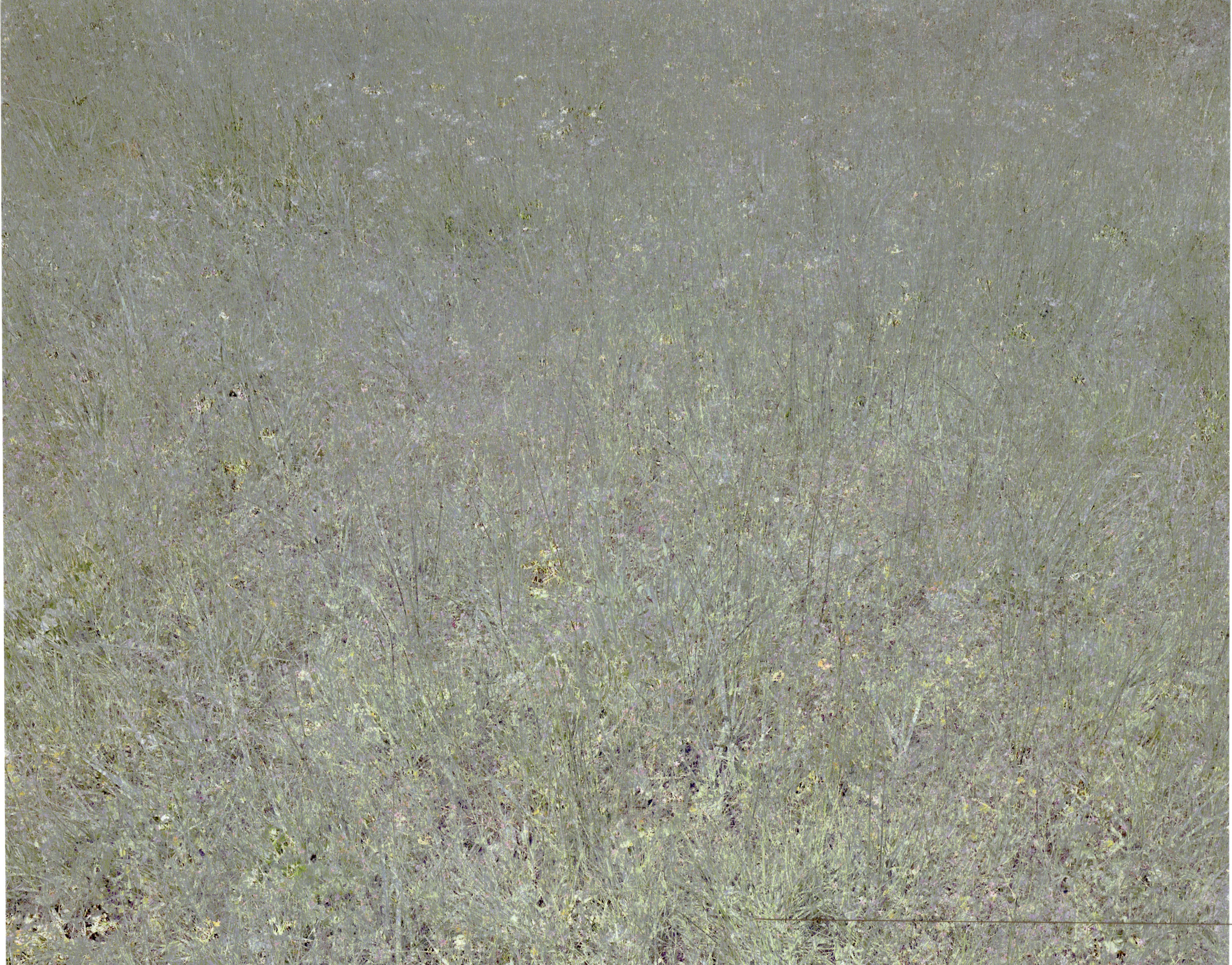

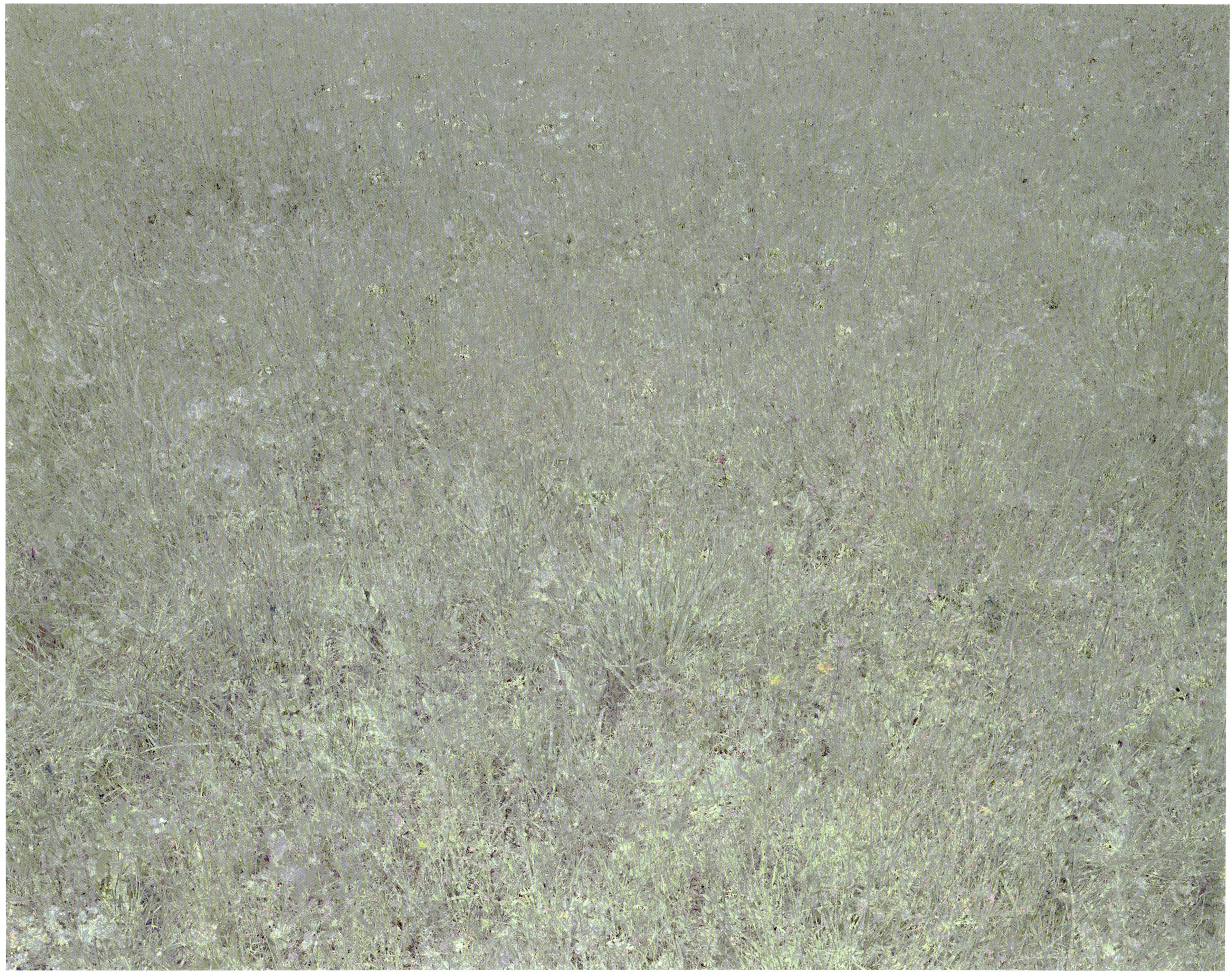

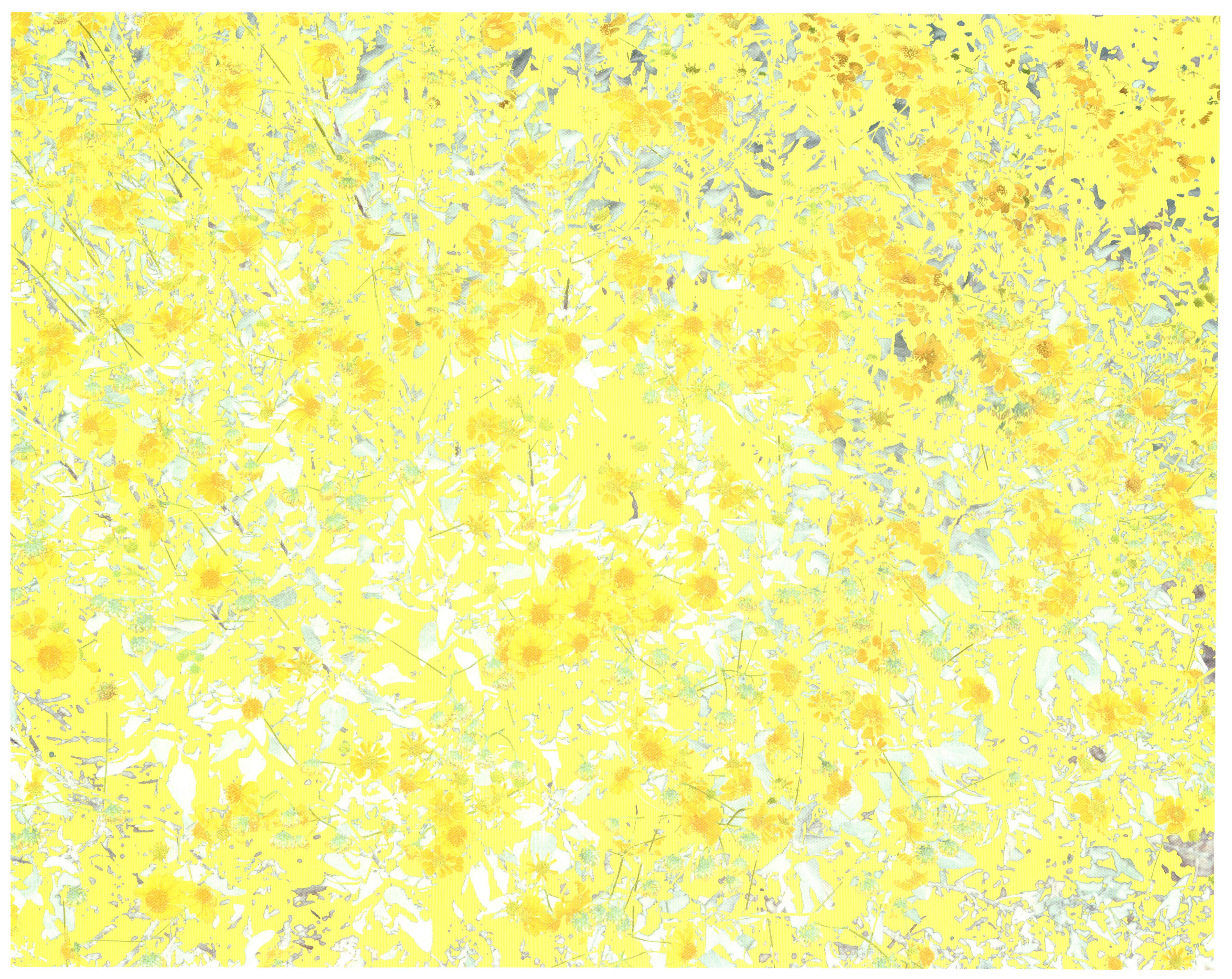

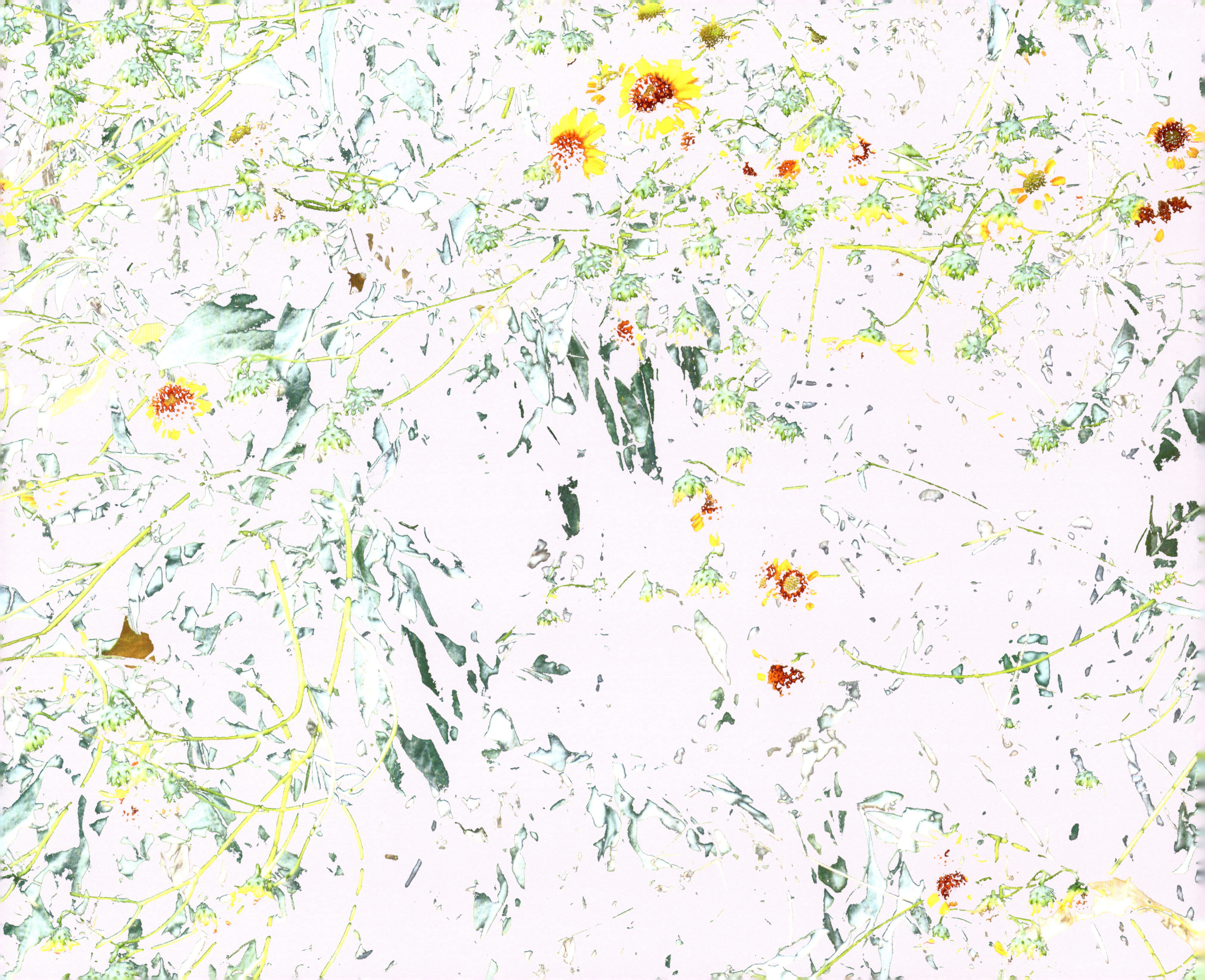

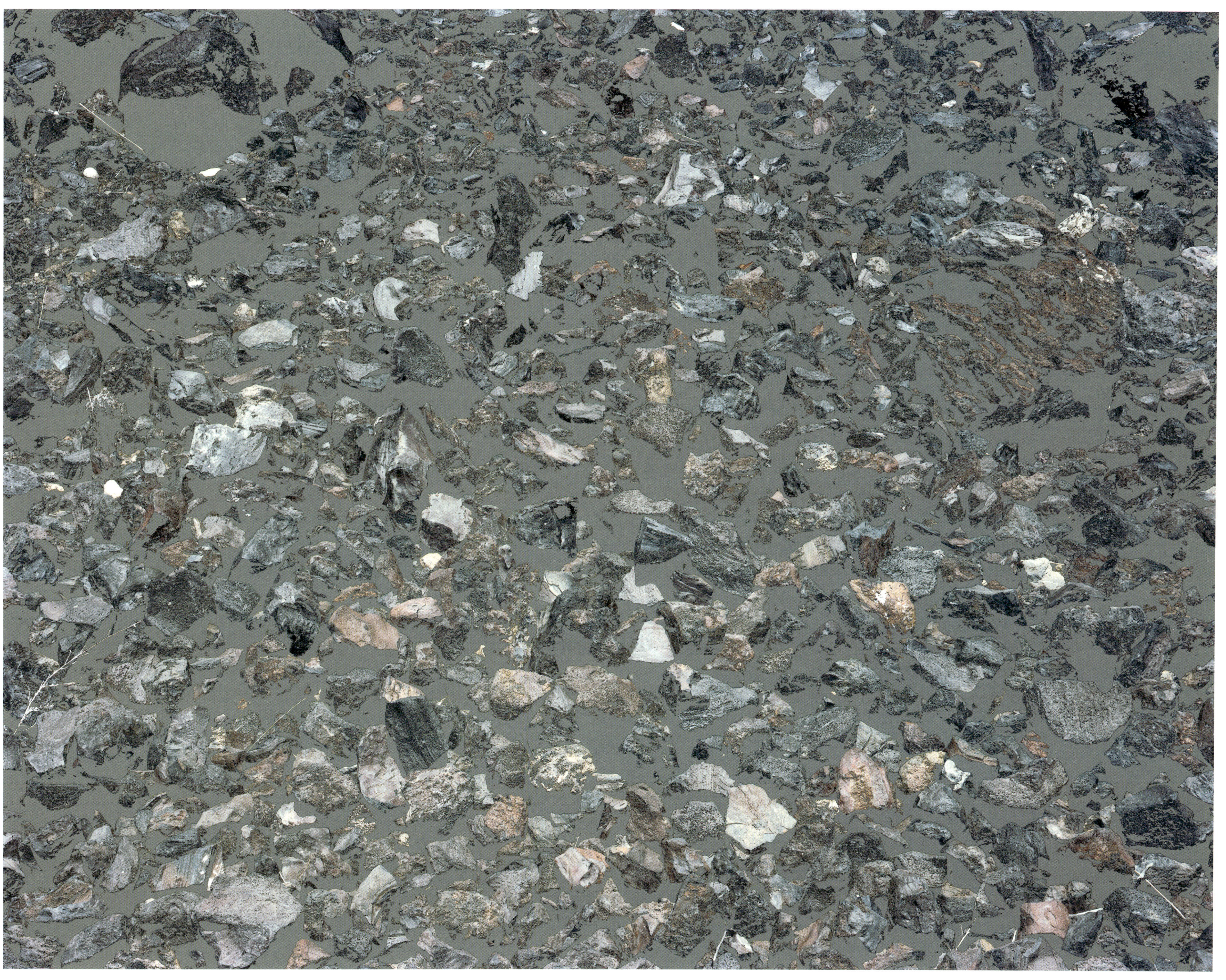

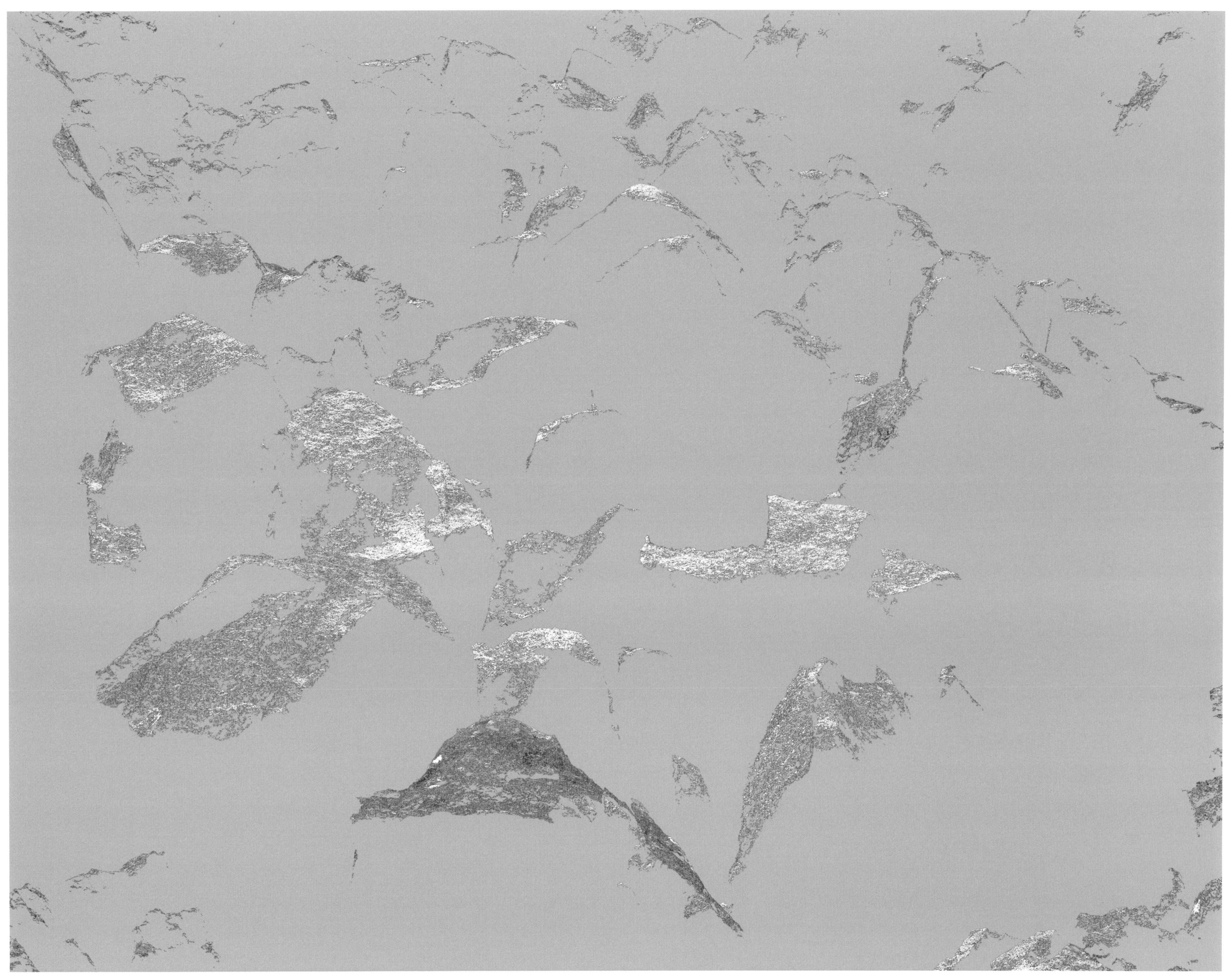

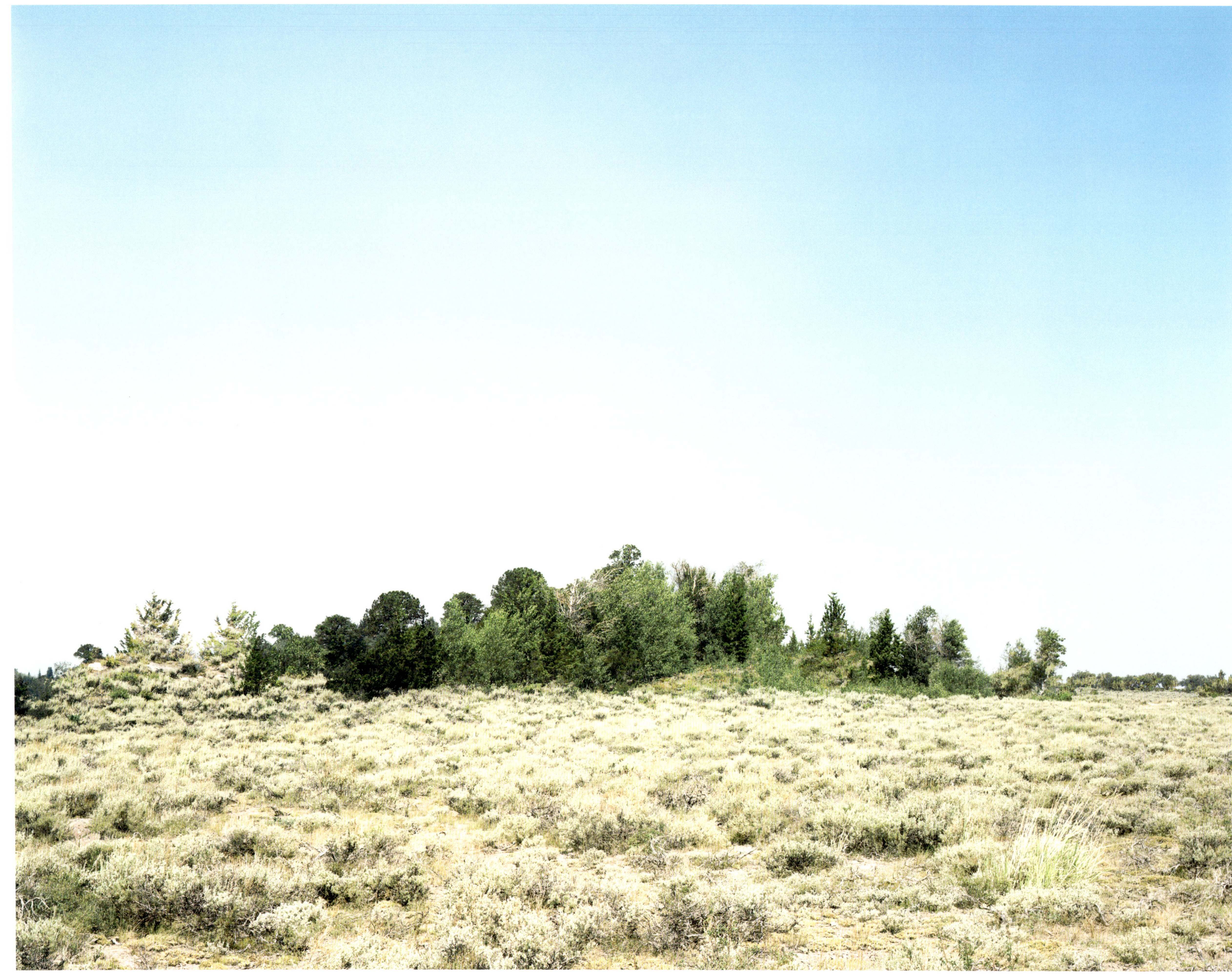

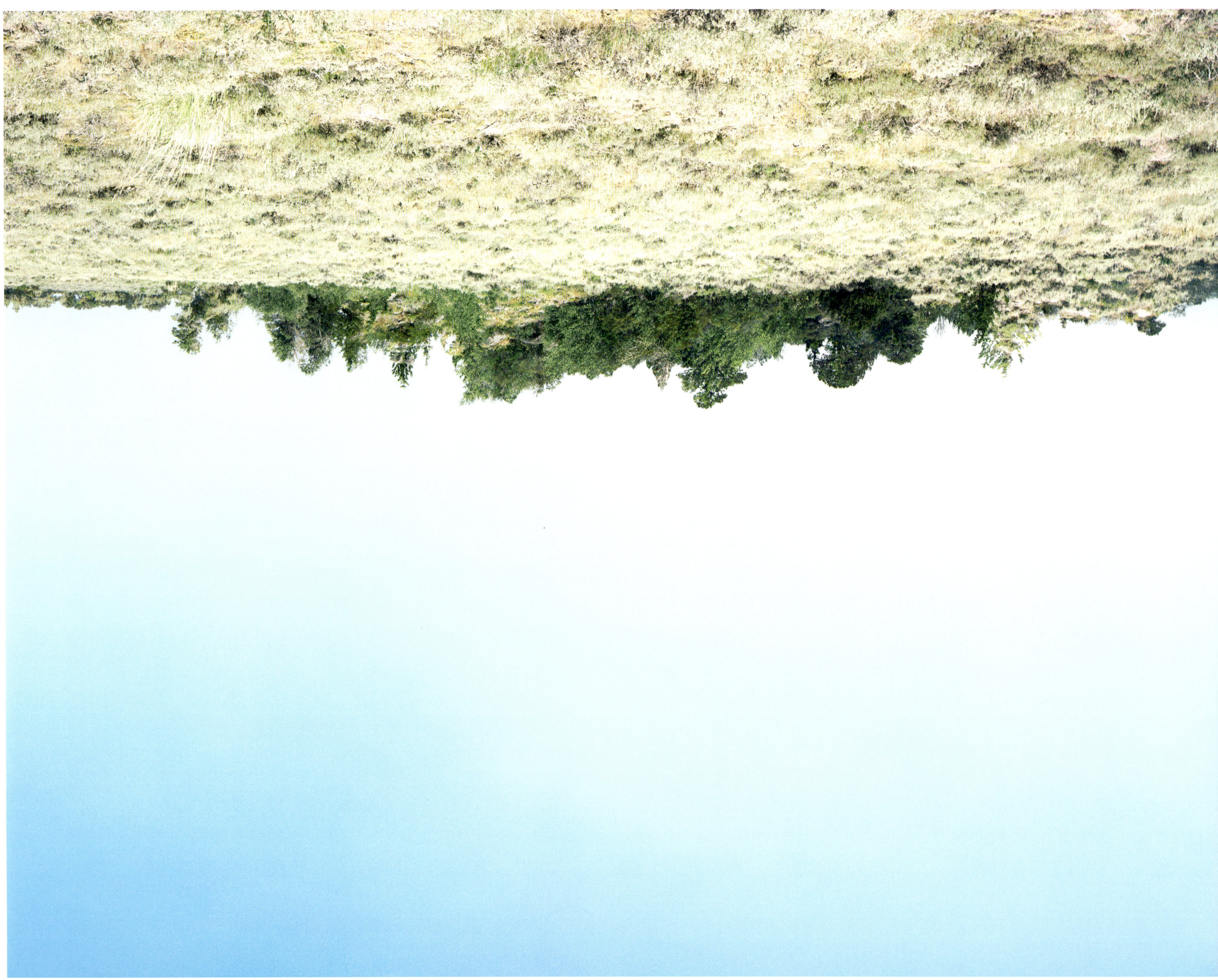

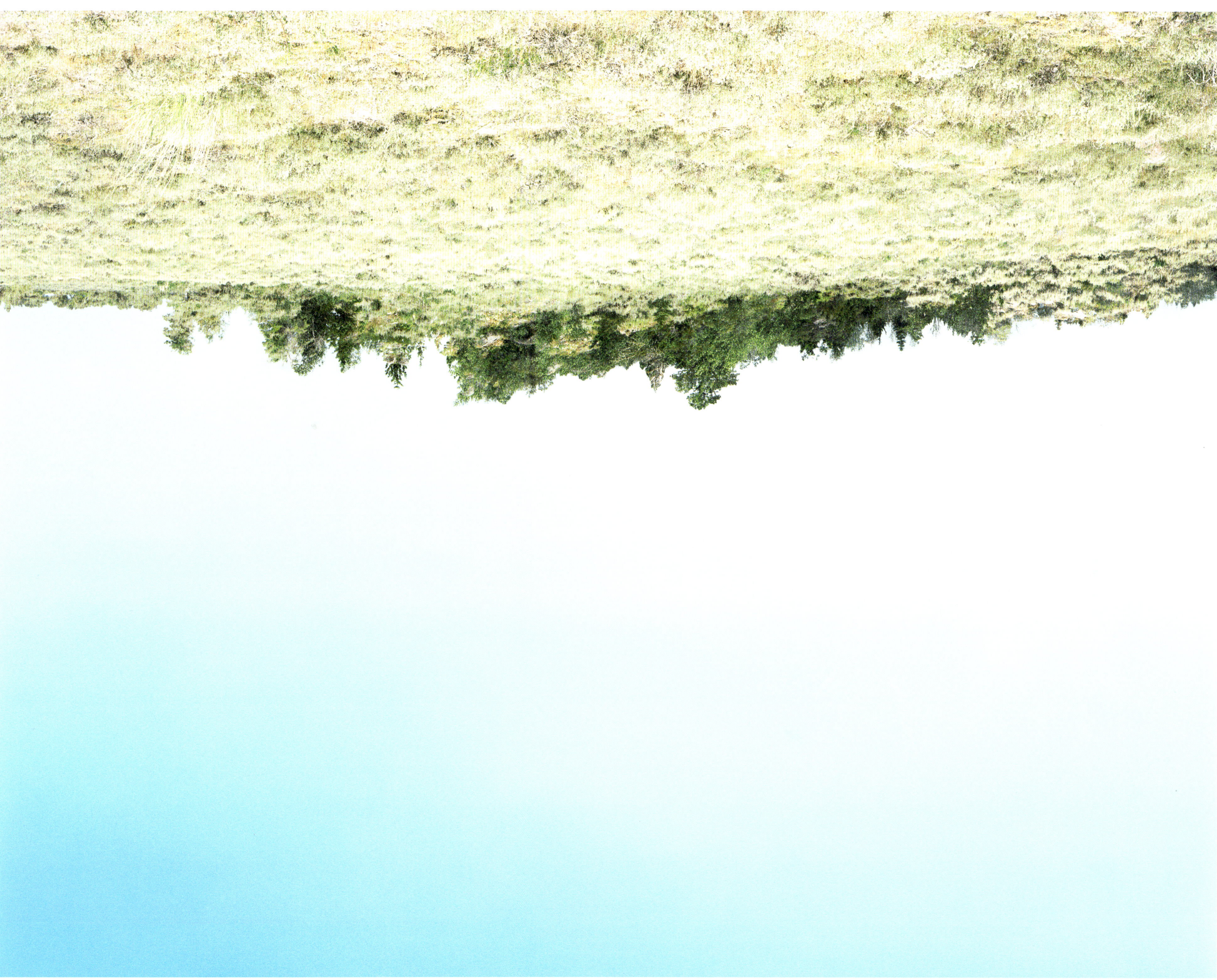

The images in this book, selected from work produced over the course of ten years, mix together a number of threads of my thought and artistic investigations. I see these different approaches as facets of a larger, open-ended exploration not defined by the specifics of technique, place, or chronology. However, I do think that it can be helpful to see how the work evolved through these overlapping approaches and groups of work. This timeline shows how the various types of work and different techniques relate to one another over the years from 2006 to 2016.

The horizontal rows separate the general digital processes I've used to create the works: the top row shows unaltered landscapes; the second row shows reversed tonalities; the third row shows multiple views layered together; the fourth row shows replaced shadows; and the bottom row shows amplified sensor noise. The images are reproduced here to scale, showing the relative print sizes of the works.

INTRODUCTION

Cassandra Coblentz

I first really got to know Aaron Rothman's work in 2009, when we worked together on an exhibition called *Looking Through the Other End of a Telescope* for the Scottsdale Museum of Contemporary Art. The exhibition explored ideas about perception relative to the camera. Central to the concept of the exhibition was an interest I have long held in the ways in which artists resist linear modes of thinking, and, in this case, use technology to attempt to depict the dynamic ways in which we perceive the world around us. This nonlinear, dynamic way of approaching the mechanisms of image production for Rothman has always been intricately connected to the components of the camera and of making a photograph. His ability to distill the essential elements of photography to their purest, most poetic essence has always astounded me.

As this book reflects back on Rothman's practice over the past decade, the depth of his nuanced study of photography and perception over this period is remarkable. Rothman's work is incredibly focused and meticulously detail-oriented, and yet simultaneously tackles broad-sweeping spaces and ideas. With each different body of work Rothman delves deeper into complex ways of recording, presenting, and considering the world in which we live, particularly the natural environment of the American West, where he is based.

Rothman's subtly nuanced consciousness of form extends beyond the creation of the photographic image itself, to the scale of the print as an object, the spatial context of an exhibition, and also to the format of a book. For this volume he developed a structure that reflects the conceptual goals of his project overall. While it comprises work made over the course of a decade, it presents a focused experience of certain overarching ideas of the work, rather than a retrospective sampling. Sequencing the images was a key factor in this endeavor, with Rothman eschewing a chronological, categorical, or stylistic ordering in favor of a nonlinear approach that draws out the dynamic relationships between his different bodies of work. For Rothman, his various bodies of work did not unfold in a clear, linear way, where one stopped and another started. Rather, they developed as parallel threads that expanded as ideas and techniques grew in relation to one another. He has always been interested in the ways in which his pictures can interact with each other and he interweaves images here in a way that lets them build on each other within the confines of the book form. The physical activity of reading or viewing this book engages an interactive impulse, encouraging one to flip back and forth between images and bodies of works.

The medium of the book also relegates the images to a mostly standard size, smaller than Rothman's prints. One particularly intriguing way Rothman has used this limitation to his advantage is in his choice of cover image. Rothman's *Cosmos* images are made as large-scale prints that relate to the viewer's physically embodied experience, and the ability to move in close to view details and also to step away to take in the entire image. Standing in front of one of these large prints, one is subsumed by the vastness and sublime beauty of the colorful image—that feeling we've all had staring up at the majesty and power of the Milky Way across a night sky. However, as one approaches the image, that grandeur dissolves into an abstraction of small patches of color, what Rothman describes as "the multi-colored confetti of noise from the camera's sensor." The viewer becomes aware that he or she is really just looking at color and light captured by the lens of a camera, rendered by a digital sensor, deftly manipulated by a computer, and printed on paper. For Rothman this dialectical experience of the image is reflective of how we take in the world.

This idea of simultaneously grappling with the micro and the macro, with the natural and the mediated, is so central to Rothman's practice that he selected a detail of the *Cosmos* photographs, *Milky Way 1*, as the cover of *Signal Noise*. He has essentially enveloped this book full of images of the vast natural world of the Western landscape with a detailed image of camera noise, the unwanted information of photography that most photographers avoid in order to present a perfectly depicted high-resolution image. Typically the aim is to have a high signal-to-noise ratio, whereby noise is the opposite of signal—something preventing clarity and understanding. However, Rothman's book title, *Signal Noise*, does not position the two words in opposition to each other, but rather sets them simply in relation to each other, side by side, working in tandem—the signal and the noise—connected in a kind of ambiguous, but harmonious way. With this singular, humble gesture, Rothman encapsulates his uncanny ability to use the material form of the photograph to create not only a heightened awareness of how we perceive, but also to somehow help us find some peace and balance in this experience, in spite of the complex world we inhabit today.

CC: When you've written about your work or described a way of anchoring it, you talk about the American West. To me, the mythologized idea of the American West is a construct of a sort that implies a way of thinking about landscape and imagery. Why is this important to you? How does the idea of a specific place play into the work?

AR: It is a specific landscape and a specific idea of landscape. I grew up in the Midwest, but I was born in California and every summer we'd go to the Sierras. It was so different from the suburban Chicago landscape, those mountains—the space and the light—and it was my favorite place to be. We also made a trip through the Arizona desert when I was young, which was a transformative experience with this immense kind of space I had never seen. I still have these kinds of experiences, and I'm still moved by the natural beauty of the West. Of course, this is complicated by all the stuff of the contemporary world and everyday life—to say nothing of the history of resource extraction and manifest destiny. I do think about the work in relation to the tradition of picturing the West, and how it breaks out of that tradition. In the end, though, this landscape is personally meaningful for me, and I work in response to that.

CC: Is this landscape one of the things that brought you to photography in the first place?

AR: I started doing photography as a teenager, mostly teaching myself through the Ansel Adams books, *The Camera*, *The Negative*, and *The Print*. These were technical books, but Adams also laid out a vision of what photography should be. I bought my 4 x 5 view camera when I was seventeen, and I brought it out to the mountains emulating that kind of work. Then I went to a college that didn't have a photo program, which pushed me down a different path. I ended up doing a lot of drawing and printmaking, all based in depicting space in an abstractive way, which had a huge influence on how I make images.

CC: Printmaking and drawing, to me, are always, in so many ways about how we see, and how we process information, and the surface of a page. You have to think spatially.

AR: I was always drawn to the back-and-forth between the flatness of the page and pictorial space. I'm not just interested in the relationship between flatness and depth, but also in the idea of figure and ground. All these dualities throughout the history of Western thought—mind and body, physical and spiritual, man and nature—play out pictorially by separating figure and ground, foreground and background. A lot of my pictures dissolve the distinction between what's foreground and what's background. While that's just a visual thing on one level, on another level, for me, it's about breaking down these binaries and this mindset that we're somehow separate from the world we inhabit.

CC: The idea of making a photograph versus taking a photograph has always interested me. Where does the process of making the image start for you? How do you think about the camera and the computer relative to each other?

AR: I think my best images always start with a real sense of connection in the moment of making the picture, and a connection to the place where it's made. This doesn't mean that the end results are about communicating that experience, though. A lot happens in the studio after I take the initial photo. I've always been fascinated by the transformative act of the photograph—how it takes the world and makes it into something else. In the past, I did a lot with traditional printing techniques to make the work more about a way of seeing or experiencing, rather than just picturing the stuff of the world. The computer is different in some ways, but I don't look at it as being categorically different. It's another layer of transformation that lets me get at certain ideas I'm interested in.

CC: So this idea of transformation is about the way we perceive? Is it the transformation of the substance of the image, in some sense?

AR: I try to use photography as a kind of metaphor for our perceptual experience. There's a world out there, and there's an experience we have in our head. Those things are connected somehow, but there's also a gap between them and we don't know exactly how they connect. In the same way, the photograph takes in the world and transmutes it into a flat image. I think this fact of photography can reveal that gap between the world and our experience of it.

CC: Let's talk more about that gap: the way we perceive imagery, and how that is different from the way we experience something. Is it even possible to articulate this difference? Is that difference a space the photograph can occupy?

AR: I think so. I can't articulate exactly what that gap is. It's a mystery of being human, never to really be resolved. But I think it comes out of our self-reflective nature. As soon as you start to reflect on any experience—as soon as you try to analyze it or get meaning out of it, or put it in memory—you put a distance to it.

CC: How do you think about time and memory relative to these works? To me, the *Pass* images
touch on those themes in a really interesting way.

AR: Those pictures compress views from over time, by combining images made over a number of years
at the same vista point in the eastern Sierras. Layering multiple images digitally, I can change how the
visual data interact to create reversals or amplifications or areas where the images cancel each other out.
I try to combine the multiple source images into one final image that feels right as its own singular
experience. For me, the pictures are partially about the distancing of memory. They are greyed out and
have a certain nostalgic feel. But they also have an ominous, digital artificiality that offsets the nostalgia.

CC: We live in such a technologically mediated world, where so much of the way we experience it is
through our screens and devices. Is this part of your interest? Does it contribute to your sense of this
distancing or this gap we talked about?

AR: It's certainly part of this work. The processes I'm using are obviously digital and the process is
always an integral part of what the work is about for me. These are landscape photographs. They're
about our relationship with the natural world, which is definitely becoming more and more mediated.
I feel like there's this shadow world of the digital realm following us around these days which is increasingly hard to get rid of, even when we're out in nature. But I don't think this virtual world that
our brains inhabit is a completely new thing. It's an expansion of our use of technology to encounter
the world, which we've done for millennia.

CC: It doesn't seem to me to be an overt criticism of this way of experiencing the world, though.
It doesn't seem like you're favoring one over the other; rather, you are presenting them as these two
parallel, or intersecting, ways of experiencing. When I look at the photographs, my first impulse is to

decipher what is real and what is virtual, to figure out how they have been manipulated. But I think it's impossible ultimately, which brings us back to that perceptual gap. The more I look at the work, though, that difference resolves itself—or at least I'm willing to let go of trying to resolve it. I'm aware of my own processing and mediating—perceiving different things simultaneously. It forces me to be open to embrace the multiple ways that we experience the world—this cross section of it all.

AR: The ambiguity of the work is a big part of it for me. We're not fixed at a point in time and space, and the world's always in flux. I want the pictures to undermine the idea that there's some perfect view or a singular vantage point on the world. The layered images combining multiple views from the same site get at this in particular. But all the work occupies these indeterminate, in-between spaces —the blurry boundary between the real and the virtual, that gap between the world and how we perceive it, and also the increasingly hard-to-make distinction between the natural and the artificial.

CC: You are not necessarily concerned with conservation per se, but there is something in the work that connects our relationship with technology to the increasingly fragile relationship we have to nature. There seems to be an impulse to preserve something real and tactile in the world. You reveal a duality between something concrete and real, and the virtual nothingness of digital information. Are you uncovering a danger in getting too comfortable in this non-material world?

AR: I'm not particularly comfortable in the immaterial digital world, but I don't go into the work trying to judge it one way or the other. I'm just trying to figure out what it's like to be in the world at this point in time. It's the same with the blurring line between natural and artificial. I think the division between the natural world and the human world has always been a false one, in a way. But, we're at a point in the history of the planet where human influence is literally everywhere. We've touched everything now, and the consequences are more and more evident. There's still beauty in nature. There's still, I think, a lot to appreciate about human presence in the world. But there's a lot to be anxious about.

CC: Is a sense of loss part of that anxiety? Because the way you play with digital information some things persist and some things disappear. You're setting up a system, using tools and technology, so that something is lost.

AR: There's definitely a lot of erasure, whether it's removing shadows or layering images in a way that obliterates the landscape. The anticipation of loss or a worry of loss is part of that.

CC: But at the same time, you're embellishing it. I think you do this in the flower images—you play with this idea of loss to create something aesthetically seductive. Can you talk about this?

AR: For those pictures, I digitally remove any part of the image that's not in direct sunlight, then fill it in with pretty, decorative colors. They kind of look like messed-up wallpaper. When I started working on them, I got interested in the history of pattern design and fabric design. As I see it, these kinds of natural motifs have been a way of reconciling our relationship with nature—to contain it, stylize it, humanize it. In my pictures, the flattening, prettifying aspect of the colors that I use plays off the chaos of the natural world, and they don't resolve into a controlled pattern. There's our impulse to contain nature and there's our inability to do so. There's a tension between those elements, but I do want the images to be genuinely pretty—and not in an ironic way. I want them to walk the line between prettiness and beauty.

CC: To me, what is interesting is that in that beauty, in that seduction of the imagery and the surface quality of the photographs, there's an underlying tension, because there is the possibility that it's all fake. Also, the fact that they have no ground, that they're unsettled as landscape, is even more potentially dystopic or threatening. The prettier it is, the more dangerous it is. We're seduced by these surface things, and there is a danger in being too drawn to insubstantial outer appearances.

AR: True enough. Being pretty or beautiful is an important part of these pictures, but there is also something more troubling. *Landscape* always refers to our construct of nature—whether it's a visual framing of it through a picture, or whether it's alteration of the land itself. There's always a bending of nature to our physical needs or conceptual desires. That has its downsides, to say the least. The prettiness of depictions of nature often devolves into sentimentality or fakeness. But behind that sentimentality, I think there's a real and valuable impulse to connect with the natural world.

CC: Do you think these images give your viewer that opportunity to connect with the natural world? Because, to me, you're putting up a barrier more than connecting to the natural world. Particularly with the erasure, at least, you're pulling them away from the natural world.

AR: There is a distancing and an obscuring of the world. If I'm in a mountain meadow where everything's in bloom, there's definitely part of me that just wants to take beautiful pictures and capture that experience. I'll try to do that, and sometimes the photos are good for what they are. But they don't really translate. There's still that distance. So giving that experience directly? No, there's no way of doing that. I'm trying to reflect on that desire to connect, and the relative inability to do so.

PLATES

All works are archival pigment prints.

ACKNOWLEDGMENTS

The work in this volume unfolded over a period of years. In that time, many people provided me with support, guidance, inspiration, and encouragement. There are a handful of individuals without whom this work wouldn't exist as it does, those who have given consistent help over the years or who have offered support and opportunities at critical moments in this work's development. Many thanks to John Mann, Mike Lundgren, and Chris Colville for always being there to give honest criticism, reassurance, and the frequent use of tools and equipment; to Cassandra Coblentz and Claire Schneider for offering crucial opportunities that emboldened me to push the work to new levels; to Rick Wester and Tom Gitterman for sage advice and helping to bring the work out to the world. Thanks also to David Chickey, Megan Mulry, Montana Currie, and Kyra Kennedy at Radius Books for all their work in making this book a reality.

Signal Noise was made possible by generous support from:

The Speranza Foundation

Martin and Toni Blume

Michelle Ho and Brett Marinoff

Chris and Jena Lohl

I also want to recognize my grandparents, Steve and Barbara Rothman, who made me into the person I am today—and who I wish were still here to see this book—and my daughter, Lia, who continually inspires me to become the person I will be tomorrow.

Most importantly, I need to express my endless love and gratitude for my partner in all of life's glories, sufferings, and mundanities. This book is dedicated to you, Rebecca.

RADIUS BOOKS is a tax-exempt 501(c)3 nonprofit organization whose mission is to encourage, promote, and publish books of artistic and cultural value. We believe that the arts play a significant role in society and that books can expand and effectively enhance great artistic vision.

RADIUS BOOKS
227 E. Palace Avenue, Suite W, Santa Fe, NM 87501 | t: (505) 983-4068 | radiusbooks.org

Available through
D.A.P. / DISTRIBUTED ART PUBLISHERS
75 Broad Street, Suite 630, New York, NY 10004 | t: (212) 627-1999 | artbook.com

ISBN 978-1-942185-35-2
Library of Congress Cataloging-in-Publication Data available from the publisher upon request

DESIGN: David Chickey & Aaron Rothman
PRE-PRESS: John Vokoun

Printed by Editoriale Bortolazzi-Stei, Verona, Italy

Cover Image: Detail of *Milky Way 1* [reproduced at original print size]

Quote by Maurice Merleau-Ponty from *The Visible and the Invisible* reproduced with permission.
Originally published in French under the title *Le Visible et l'invisible*. Copyright © 1964 by Editions Gallimard, Paris.
English translation copyright © 1968 by Northwestern University Press. First printing 1968. All rights reserved.

Quote from "(Nothing But) Flowers" used with permission from Alfred Music.
Words and music by David Byrne, Jerry Harrison, Christopher Frantz, Tina Weymouth & Yves Njock.
Copyright © 1988 Index Music, Inc. (ASCAP), All rights administered by WB Music Corp. All rights reserved.